Why Are the Arabs Not Free? –
The Politics of Writing

Why Are the Arabs Not Free? –
The Politics of Writing

MOUSTAPHA SAFOUAN

Blackwell
Publishing

BLACKWELL PUBLISHING
350 Main Street, Malden, MA 02148-5020, USA
9600 Garsington Road, Oxford, OX4 2DQ, UK
550 Swanston Street, Carlton, Victoria 3053, Australia

First published 2007 by Blackwell Publishing Ltd

Library of Congress Cataloging-in-Publication Data

Safouan, Moustafa.
  Why are the Arabs not free? : the politics of writing / Moustapha Safouan.
   p. cm.
  Includes bibliographical references and index.
  ISBN 978-1-4051-6171-8 (pbk. : alk. paper) 1. Arab countries–Politics and government–20th century. 2. Arab countries–Intellectual life–20th century. 3. Civilization, Arab–20th century. I. Title.

  DS39.S237 2007
  320.17′4927–dc22

                          2007010860

A catalogue record for this title is available from the British Library.

Set in 10 on 13 pt Palatino
by Macmillan India
Printed and bound in the United Kingdom
by Charlesworth

The publisher's policy is to use permanent paper from mills that operate a sustainable forestry policy, and which has been manufactured from pulp processed using acid-free and elementary chlorine-free practices. Furthermore, the publisher ensures that the text paper and cover board used have met acceptable environmental accreditation standards.

For further information on
Blackwell Publishing, visit our website:
http://www.blackwellpublishing.com

In memoriam

Mohammed Auda

1920–2006

Contents

Acknowledgements

The first drafts of this book, except for the final chapter, were written in Arabic for a variety of purposes: articles, conferences, introductions. It was Dr Hussein Abdelkader who had the idea of publishing them as a book in Egypt. Unable to find a publisher willing to take the responsibility for such a book, he published it himself using the fictitious cover of a publisher specialising in clinical psychology, which enabled him to obtain the censor's authorisation. He publicised the book by sending it to a wide circle of his friends: journalists, men of letters, artists, teachers. lawyers et cetera. Apart from an appreciative response from Gamal Elghitany, the book elicited no reaction.

After hearing a draft of the final chapter on the structure of political power in the Middle East at a London Consortium/University of Pittsburgh seminar in September 2002 and learning that it was the continuation of the arguments contained in the book published by Dr Hussein Abdelkader, Colin MacCabe obtained a report on the book from Dr Ronald Judy of the University of Pittsburgh which strongly recommended publication in English. The report also stressed that the book would pose particular problems of translation as half of it was written in Egyptian demotic and half in classical Arabic, languages which the book itself argues are as different as Italian and Latin.

The translation was entrusted, on the recommendation of Dr Mounir Shamoun, to the Department of Translation of St Joseph University, Beirut. This translation, however, needed to be widely revised and enlarged in order to adapt it for non-Arab readers. This revision was guided and constantly stimulated by the critical remarks and suggestions of Colin Mac-Cabe who, moreover, undertook a final English redaction of the whole book.

The English text presented here owes its existence a second time to Dr Hussein Abdelkader who furnished me with all the Arabic sources I needed, almost all of which had been out of print for many decades. He also provided me with many documents from the archives of Al-Azhar university and other religious institutions. More than that, however, and in answer to questions about key matters such as the relation between the temporal and spiritual powers in the Islamic state, he sent me his own studies on these questions, generously allowing me to make use of them as I saw fit. My debt to him and to Colin MacCabe is so great that I consider this book, as it now stands, to be a team effort.

Foreword

Derrida has taught us that it is impossible to give an origin to a text. Language is so intricate a web that, at its limit, each word is every word, caught in a network of meanings that only the God of Abraham could comprehend in its totality. But if with Aristotle we turn from theory to evidence, then in one important sense we can locate this book's beginning precisely in both time and place. The time was 9 June 1967 and the place Paris.

On 9 June 1967 Gamal Abdel Nasser addressed the people of Egypt by radio. It is difficult now to recall the kind of prestige that Nasser had enjoyed before that June. He had been the mastermind of the army's July plot which toppled the unloved and unlovely Egyptian monarchy in 1952. He was the hero of Suez who in 1956 had faced down both British and French imperialism, the powers which had divided the world for more than two centuries. He had with Tito and Nehru inaugurated at Bandung in 1957 the movement of non-aligned countries which offered to the countries emerging from colonial domination an alternative to a single choice between Soviet communism and American capitalism.

In the spring of 1967, however, he had made a fatal error as he mimicked the actions of a country about to declare war. The Israelis needed no better excuse to unleash their superior weapons and organisation and Nasser found himself the loser in a catastrophic war which he had provoked. Five days after the war had begun, Egypt's forces had been comprehensively defeated and Nasser took to the airwaves to announce his resignation.

This event, with its tragic origin and farcical conclusion – millions of Egyptians poured onto the streets to persuade their beloved leader to remain as their guide and protector – made clear to Moustapha Safouan, an Egyptian psychoanalyst living in Paris, that the problem of despotism was a problem which the Third World in general, and Arab peoples in particular, needed to confront. In taking Arab despotism as a problem to be analysed, Safouan was differentiating himself from the quasi totality of the Western left, who conceived Arab despotism as the responsibility either of historic colonialism or of contemporary imperialism. As an Egyptian whose father had been one of the founders of the Egyptian Communist party, Safouan was unwilling to accept this patronising refusal to confront the failures of national liberation. Furthermore, as a psychoanalyst, he could see all too clearly how despotism was from a psychic perspective a very satisfactory political settlement.

Safouan, who came from his native Alexandria to Paris at the end of the Second World War, was one of the first of Lacan's pupils. Safouan was there in 1951 when Lacan started his first seminars with an audience that could fit into his consulting rooms. Two decades later these seminars were huge public events with an audience of thousands. By that time it was difficult to understand how anybody could be Lacan's pupil, for Lacan had abandoned the position of teacher for that of celebrity. But Safouan encountered Lacan at a time when the force of his teaching was such that Safouan has not only compared him to Socrates, but compared him favourably, for he holds the Parisian psychoanalyst superior to the Athenian thinker because of Lacan's greater skill in compelling his students to realise that the truth he was articulating could not be identified with his person. Specifically, Lacan's distinction between the imaginary father of intersubjective relations and the symbolic father of the social order enabled Safouan to resolve the paradoxes of Freud's own incomplete elaboration of the Oedipus complex. In the Freudian account, the rivalry with the father is brought to an end by the son accepting the father's dominance, but this acceptance is both too conscious and insufficiently necessary. Lacan's genius is to differentiate between the rivalry with the all-powerful father that occurs at the imaginary level and the recognition that the father himself is not the all-powerful cause of his own desire, but is himself articulated within a symbolic order which he does not control. This recognition that the father is no more than a name, the privileged sign of the arbitrary power of language, is Lacan's theorisation of the Freudian concept of castration.

This theoretical clarification has consequences for politics. All the experience of psychoanalysis testifies to the power of the narcissism that attaches to the first stage of this process, when the figure of the father as rival holds out the hope of an uncastrated being. Indeed, at the end of his life, in his paper on the interminable nature of psychoanalysis, Freud identified the narcissistic rejection of femininity as the deepest resistance to analysis in male patients. But it is for this deepest resistance that the despot is such a satisfactory figure. Indeed one might reflect that, from the point of view of psychoanalysis, it is democracy and not despotism that is difficult to explain.

Safouan's determination to confront the question of Arab despotism after 9 June 1967 thus had two clear and distinct components. On the one hand it was the reaction of someone who had been raised in the struggle for national independence and could see clearly how the dreams of that struggle had evaporated with dispiriting rapidity, but it was also the reaction of a Lacanian psychoanalyst who knew both theoretically and practically the power of the figure of the imaginary father.

Safouan himself describes how in his first efforts he turned to the sixteenth-century thinker Etienne de la Boétie and the first chapter of this book is based on the introduction to his translation into Arabic of la Boétie's *Discourse on Voluntary Servitude*. This chapter is an astonishing summary of much of the work of the Annales school of historians who were such an important part of the intellectual ferment of the inter-war years in Paris and were perhaps a neglected element in the flowering of the sixties – it is very difficult indeed to imagine the work of Michel Foucault, for example, without the efforts of these historians. Safouan summarises this work for an Arab audience but, as his purpose is to explain the dominance of the West over the Arab world in modern times, he does more than summarise; he also indicates those elements which he considers vital in the transformation of Western Europe from the backwardness of the Dark Ages – in which Rome was indeed a dark city compared to the brilliance of Byzantium and Baghdad – to the dominance of the modern era. Safouan's is a materialist but not a Marxist history. Trade and the growth of a money economy are crucial elements in Europe's increasing power but, for Safouan, institutions are the key moment where new psychic forces become material power. The two vital institutions, both unique to medieval Europe, are the corporation – a body whose legal existence outlives any particular member – and the university, a corporation which finds its common activity not in metalwork or the manufacture of clothes but in the investigation of knowledge.

It is common today to hear the call for interdisciplinarity; no government research body or university worth its salt fails to declare its commitment to research which covers more than one discipline. However, in all Western countries the ever-increasing bureaucratisation of learning means that the disciplines become stronger and stronger in their isolation. The result is a situation where literary departments practise a literary interdisciplinarity, historians a historians' version, and anthropology and sociology come up with an account for social scientists. Safouan undertakes the real thing. The position of psychoanalyst meant that he pursued his studies unconstrained by the professional divisions of the disciplines. It is this position which enables him to range so freely from history to political philosophy to theology without having to assert the primacy of one over the other. Safouan also enjoyed a privilege which is not now accorded to any academic, no matter how brilliant. As a psychoanalyst there was little professional requirement to publish and indeed the translation of de la Boétie was not undertaken until he was very nearly 50. The introduction to that work testifies to an extraordinary period of development, to a slow time of reading and reflection.The productivity of that slow time can be appreciated on every page of this book.

If one can date the beginning of this book to 1967, it is more difficult to isolate the moment at which Safouan elaborated his solution to the problem of Arab despotism although it could be noticed that the seventies and eighties, including the disastrous development of Arafat's leadership of the Palestinians, made that problem ever more evident. For Safouan, the analysis of the corporation and the university, however key they were to Western development, did not provide an answer to the question of how a people acquiesced in their own servitude. In fact that original question was fast transforming, because psychoanalysis and the power of the imaginary father made despotism almost a natural condition and made it clear that the real question was: what were the symbolic conditions that enabled the growth of democracy? The undoubted starting point of Safouan's answer to this questions were the reflections on writing and power in Levi Strauss's *Tristes Tropiques* which were so intellectually fertile in the fifties and sixties. Also important was the period in the late eighties and early nineties when Safouan bought a house on the Red Sea to which he hoped to retire and from which he re-engaged directly with Egyptian intellecuual and cultural life. This period confirmed the closed nature of the intellectual world of classical Arabic and the fact that Arab despotism was dependent on the use of writing as a means of power and exploitation. The final step came with the publication of Adonis's great poem *The Book* (*al-Kitab*) when it was clear that even such a revolutionary work could not break the closed linguistic circle. It was at this point that Safouan decided to follow the satirists and the love poets and to write in demotic Egyptian.

It is uncomfortable for any academic to write a foreword to a book which he cannot read in its original language, but it is almost ludicrous to say anything about a book which I cannot read in any language. Adonis's *The Book* was widely acknowledged as a masterpiece when it was first published in 1995, and translations are in progress in both French and English, but for the moment I know of it only by report. For Safouan, however, it clearly marked a decisive moment in his understanding of the role of classical Arabic. In particular, it was on reading this poem that Safouan recognised that classical Arabic was, like Latin and Greek, a dead language, a point that Adonis himself has stressed in commenting on his own poem.

This insight leads us to the central thesis of this book, which can be summarised as follows. The classical Arabic in which all formal education is conducted in Arab countries is a dead language which differs as much from the spoken Arabic of Egypt, Morocco and the Gulf States as Latin differs from Italian. Moreover, the spoken languages, the demotics, of Egypt, Morocco and the Gulf States differ from each other as much as do Italian, Spanish and French. Thus the written language, the language of culture and learning, is completely divorced from the language of the common people. This situation is not, as we might think, unusual, for if we look at the history of despotism in Egypt, a history which goes back over 5,000 years, we find that writing has always occupied this privileged position and indeed we can begin to realise that despotism has as a necessary condition a written language which is limited to an elite entirely at the service of power. If we compare this state of affairs, common in the Mediterranean from the beginning of civilisation to the present day, with Athens and the beginnings of democracy in the fifth century BC, we will find that what is unusual about Athens is that writing is in the demotic and is publicly available. At this point it becomes clear that what the West needed to add to the institutions of the corporation and the university in order to become the dominant global power were systems of writing and education which were in the demotic. The process by which Europe transformed itself from a polity in which writing was limited to an archaic language and a special caste to one in which writing in the vernacular was available to all is called, for shorthand, the Reformation, which itself built on the scholarly and literary achievements of the Renaissance. On Safouan's account the crucial feature of the Reformation is that a language which because it is dead will always be identified with the masculine setting in which it is taught is replaced by writing in mother tongues. It is this writing with mother tongues which enables the European polities to engage the full energy of their people and to escape from the awful tutelage of despotism. Linguistic humanism, the decision of Dante to write *The Divine Comedy* in the vernacular, the determination of Martin Luther to translate the Bible into German, this is the key to Europe's extraordinary global success

Safouan's thesis is so powerful at least in part because it is so surprising and so controversial in its very facts. When I was considering publishing this book I had several conversations about Safouan's thesis with Arabs who held eminent positions in American universities. There were some who simply denied, and denied in the strongest and most emotional terms, the linguistic facts that Safouan appealed to. It is possible to explain this reaction both by the attachment, about which Safouan writes so movingly, that any educated Arab has to the classical tongue in which he or she has been taught, but also in terms of the still influential ideology of pan-Arabism which depends for much of its appeal on the assertion that all Arabs speak the same language.

It is not surprising that modern linguistics has nothing to say about the fascinating linguistic situation which Safouan describes, because modern linguistics has no conception whatsoever of a national language. There is a classic joke, deployed in Linguistics 101, which says that a language is a dialect with an army and navy. The joke makes clear that in dealing with questions of national language we are dealing directly with politics, with the ways in which a language reproduces itself, exactly the question of Safouan's book. Modern linguistics, over a century ago, set itself up by divorcing itself from all such questions of value. If we look at the Chomskyan linguistics which has been such a powerful intellectual force over the past half-century, we can see that while it does require the notion of a language in order to constitute its corpus – of any sentence it must be possible to say whether it is well formed within the language or not – this notion is located at the level of the individual speaker's competence. Chomsky, and indeed all other schools of modern linguistics, are unable to deal with the kind of situation Safouan describes, in which any educated speaker of Arabic is effectively operating with two different competences: one a standard related to the apparatus of schools and publication and the second related to speech and everyday life.

Theoretically, of course, linguistics does not even entertain as a question the range of variation that can be found within a national standard, as Arjuna Parakrama demonstrates in *De-Hegemonizing*

Language Standards: Learning from (Post) Colonial Englishes about 'English'.[1] Almost all the arguments which have historically been used to delegitimate colonial variants of English have no basis in linguistics because there is no notion of how much variation a language can maintain without losing its very intercommunicability. This theoretical question presses at the very limit of the human; closer to earth it makes it easy to understand how the linguistic situation that Safouan describes can both obtain and be denied by native speakers.

When the war ended, Safouan had determined to set out for Cambridge and the study of logic. The vicissitudes of foreign scholarships saw him arrive in Paris rather than Cambridge. But it could fairly be said that the love of logic has never left Safouan, and his arguments move from few premises with a limited number of variables to their certain conclusions. It may be necessary, however, to complicate the variables without losing the elegance of the argument form. The first variable that we might need to add to the thesis that Safouan proposes is the notion of medium. In the universe of Safouan's politics of writing, we deal with the spoken word and the written book, but almost all of the world's major languages have been developed in recent decades through the various modern mass media: the press, radio and television. There seems little doubt that these forms offer intermediate stages between the universal classical Arabic of the school and the particular demotic of this or that country. This also offers a caution to the contrast of a West which enjoys full participation in its symbolic reproduction with an Arab world deprived of any significant voice except that of its corrupt and despotic rulers. Faced with a choice between Saddam Hussein and Rupert Murdoch, it is not difficult to choose the press baron, but this choice makes clear how limited notions of freedom of expression are for much of the West.

A second and as significant a variable is gender. Safouan's account of the distinction between an elite and arcane writing identified with an omnipotent father and a bounteous mother-tongue available to the totality of the population has a force and a sense which we should not lose sight of. But the reality of European history makes for a much more complicated and nuanced reading of this opposition. The linguistic humanism which Safouan so prizes was constantly developed in relation to Latin. Margaret Ferguson's *Dido's Daughters* argues that it is impossible to understand European vernacular literacy in this period unless one understands any particular vernacular in relation to Latin.[2] This bilingual situation is even more complicated in England where, well into the fifteenth century, three languages are in play,

Latin, English and French. Ferguson argues convincingly that Renaissance valorisations of the vernacular are dominantly calqued on Latin. To attain to the cultural authority of Latin, a vernacular must not only be written, it must also be extracted from the female-dominated setting of the house to the male-dominated setting of the school. The gendering of literacy is not simply a question of who has access to literacy, it is a question of how particular literacy practices are ideologically gendered.

As with the question of medium, consideration of gender may multiply the variables but it does not necessarily contradict the basic argument. Indeed, to take the basic argument further would require concrete studies on the relations between the spoken and the written in contemporary Arabic as well as in other countries and languages around the world.

In introducing a book which is so sensitive to the play of language, a necessary insensitivity must be confessed. Safouan's original text was published in two different languages – the classical Arabic that he used for la Boétie and his early translations of Hegel and Freud, and the demotic Egyptian in which he developed his theory of the vernacular and into which he translated Shakespeare's *Othello*. No effort has been made to reproduce this linguistic variation in a translation which has limited its ambition to a rendering of Safouan's arguments into good modern English.

Safouan's theses about the relation between classical and demotic in Arabic have fascinated me since I first heard them in conversation. It was, however, a post-9/11 world which made their publication in English seem an urgent task. When I undertook that task almost five years ago, I had no idea of the difficulties of translating and publishing a book originally written in Arabic. The automatic channels which provide translators and publishers for books in other European languages simply do not exist, and the experience has made it all too clear to me that many of the material conditions for the dialogue between civilisations which our political masters say they desire are completely absent. At the same time, Safouan's text seemed to offer a perfect example of the way in which theoretical reflection and political analysis may illuminate each other, and to prove, if proof were needed, how our very being is linguistic. As such it was a perfect choice to inaugurate a series of *Critical Quarterly* books that will attempt to carry the concerns of the magazine into a new form.

In his introduction, Safouan talks of the teamwork which has brought this book into being. Two further members have been added to the team in the final stages. Francis Gooding tracked quotations and bibliographic references through several languages and Joanna Jellinek brought her superb grasp of written English to the improvement of the text still further. The fate of any book is uncertain, particularly in a world so inundated with information. However, in working on this text I have had the sensation of overhearing a conversation in another culture which is of immediate importance for our own. There can be few ideas more inspiring in the contemporary world than that of the Caliphate. The desire to believe in a better world, in a city on the hill, seems as fundamental as any human desire. The secular promises of socialism and consumerism have both proved empty in their different ways. The desire for social justice, so strong in the Prophet's message, finds a ready slogan in the notion of a global community. However, the Prophet's message was so strong because of the unique position he occupied between a tribal and a commercial way of life. This uniqueness is recognised by Islam; indeed it is one of its very core beliefs. The Prophet's relation to God was unique, and he can have no successor. The question of what Islam means politically in the modern era is an open one.

COLIN MACCABE
November 2006

Notes

1 Arjuna Parakrama, *De-Hegemonizing Language Standards: Learning from (Post) Colonial Englishes about 'English'* (Basingstoke: Macmillan, 1995).

2 Margaret W. Ferguson, *Dido's Daughters: Literacy, Gender, and Empire in Early Modern England and France* (Chicago: Chicago University Press, 2003), 83–134.

Introduction

I began this book almost forty years ago and at that time I had no idea whatever about the relation between writing and power. I started writing it in the aftermath of the Six Day War defeat, in June 1967, which I understood as part of a much more general and comprehensive defeat of the Third World, apart from India.

It is true that the West fought unremittingly against liberation movements in the Third World, without any consideration for legal or humanitarian principles. But it is just as true that, except in India, political power was monopolised in the Third World countries by one ruler. No voice other than his was to be heard, nor could any opinion other than his be expressed; anyone daring to dissent could expect no possible fate but jail or death.

Moreover, although the word 'liberation' aroused great passions among the masses, passions which can still be felt in the writings of Frantz Fanon, the word itself merely named a goal; that is, freedom from colonialism and/or from the political pressure of the two great powers of that epoch. However, the word afforded no clue as to how that liberation was to be achieved, nor what to do with it if it was achieved.

The 'hypnotic power of the master words', to borrow a friend's expression, and my puzzlement at the monopolisation of political power came together in my decision to translate into Arabic a text that had first appeared in 1530 in France, where it is known as *The Discourse on Voluntary Servitude*, by Etienne de la Boétie. This discourse has been revived on many occasions, most often during times of political agitation, and it has remained widely read. Revolutionary groups called it *Contre l'Un* – Against the One. La Boétie's aim was to understand how one man, the 'Monarch', can reduce millions of subjects to slavery. It was inevitable that his essay would have a deep impact on me.

I was born and brought up in a country, Egypt, which was a British protectorate. Gladstone, who gave the British fleet the order to bombard Alexandria in 1870, considered the occupation of that country to be a work of civilisation. One might say, with a grain of salt, that he had a point. The British introduced to the Middle East, for the first time in its millennial history, two notions that not only had never been heard of before; they had never even been dreamt of: the separation of powers and democracy. 'The three powers, legislative, executive and judiciary, on whose separation the modern state is built, were concentrated under the absolute regimes in the same dominating hand that controlled all public affairs. The Islamic state was no exception.'[1] It is true that the three spheres of activity, legislation, execution and judgement, were distinguished. But this distinction remained purely theoretical. 'In practice, these activities, corresponding to the three powers in the modern state, always interfered with each other and were always submitted, whether separately or *ensemble*, to the opinion of the Caliph, Sultan or Emir. This opinion was above all law, judgement or discipline, although it tried most of the time to have a *semblance* of legitimacy.'[2] To provide such a *semblance* was not a hard matter. It is true that the judges acquired their prestige from the Koran and the judicial tradition, but, except in the few cases which depended on the character of the judge and not on the nature of the regime, the caliph could always get the interpretation of the text that suited him best. This was all the easier as there was no supreme court with the necessary guarantees of independence. Judges were subject to dismissal or replacement and were responsible to the caliph.[3] In brief, the celestial drama of the last judgement was played as an *Ubu*-esque farce on earth.

As to democracy, it would be absurd to think that it was in order to ease the class struggle that the British introduced political parties to a country like Egypt where social hierarchy and differences of status were always considered as natural facts dependent on God's will. Most probably, the introduction of the political parties was an application of the motto: 'Divide and rule.' However, an utterly new vocabulary was introduced: constitution, representation, elections, parties, parliament, majority, minority, and so forth. It is true that the parties did not represent effective social currents, with the exception of the Wafd party which incarnated the common aspiration to independence. There was also the Muslim Brothers party, founded in March 1928 by Hassan Albanna, who used the name of God in order to recruit the support that could transform that name into a political or temporal power. But this party was illegal according to the state because, as the constitution stipulated that the state itself was Islamic, it saw an *Islamic* party simply as an enemy questioning its own legitimacy. All other parties were considered to be the creation either of the

British High Commissioner or of the Royal Palace. In brief, words did not create facts. But they did create modes of thought that it would not be an exaggeration to qualify as revolutionary. For the first time in the history of the land, a serious deliberation began, thanks to Mohammad Abdou, 'the father of Muslim reform', with a view to adapting Islam to the exigencies of modern times; movements for the liberation of women saw the light of day thanks to Qassem Amin. Ali Abdelrazek questioned for the first time whether the whole idea of the caliph, or successor, had any secure basis in Islam. This attack on the notion of a single legitimate successor to the Prophet, which has been so significant in Islamic history, was all the more subversive as King Fouad, who was appointed by the British, wanted to acquire further legitimacy by being considered a descendant of the Prophet and, therefore, as a caliph or successor. The 'council of honourable "ulamaa"' (savants), composed of twenty-four members, headed by the dean of Al-Azhar, the greatest university of Islamic studies in the Muslim world, held a court of inquiry on 12 August 1925 and decided unanimously to deprive Ali Abdelrazek of his title as 'alem or doctor, and to forbid him from exercising any office either as a teacher or a judge. Taha Hussein published a book in 1926 on pre-Islamic poetry, in which he considered the Koran as a great work of art which reflected the social life on the Arabic peninsula at the time of Mohammed better than any other source. Once again the dean of Al-Azhar sent to the attorney general a report written by the doctors of the university accusing Hussein of blasphemy and other similar charges. The attorney general fully admitted that the doctors' criticism was completely well founded, but, noting that the author, though without criminal intention, merely wrote what he believed – wrongly – to be the truth, he dismissed the case. It is worth recognising that no Muslim state nowadays would allow the publication of these books and that their publication would actually endanger the lives of their authors at the hands of the fundamentalists. In that moment of intellectual ferment, works of Darwin and Marx were also translated. Thanks to Ahmad Amin, the Committee for Writings, Translations and Publishing was created, to which we owe some of the best translations written in Arabic – anyone of my age still remembers the deep poetic emotions aroused by Fakhry Abulsu'oud's incomparable translation of Thomas Hardy's *Tess*. Indeed, this was the last period to witness great writing in classical Arabic, and many of us owe our attachment to, not to say veneration of, that language to the fact that it was, as my old friend Mohammad Auda said, 'the language of our national movement'.

I left Egypt for France at the beginning of January 1946. The national movement continued with more vigour after the war. While the British were keen to keep the Suez Canal and to maintain their control with a military force, they were prepared to leave the rest of the country when the so-called revolution of 23 July 1952 took place. In fact, this was no revolution but a military coup d'état in the style that was familiar in the banana republics. From the very first day the bunch of officers who fomented it launched a slogan composed of three words which, far from reflecting the people's aspirations, such as 'liberty, fraternity and equality', had the unmistakable smell of the superego: 'unity, discipline and work'. Shortly after the coup d'état a strike took place in a textile factory in a small town near Alexandria (Kafr Eldawar). Two workers were publicly hanged. This was a remarkable commentary on the triple slogan: unity in terror; discipline in slavery; work or death. But the astonishing thing was the rapidity and ease with which the advances of the nationalist movement were nullified. Sixty university professors, including the great writer and eminent critic Lewis Awad, were fired at one stroke, which practically amounted to putting an end to all higher education in the country; great writers were marginalised; Ahmad Amin's *Committee for Writings, Translations and Publishing* disappeared; the press and the publishing houses were nationalised. This was not all. Political parties were abolished and the existence of a multi-party system denounced as the source of all evil; opposition was savagely repressed: the communists, who never amounted to a force dangerous to the state, were tortured, imprisoned or removed to camps in the desert; the Muslim Brothers suffered the same fate, although in their case the government's fears were more justified.

I had left Alexandria, the city in which I was born and educated, and gone to Europe without ever truly knowing my country – I had no idea about life in the countryside and I had to all intents and purposes never encountered the figure to whom Egypt owes its material existence, its very being: the peasant (*fallah*).

Moreover, I had a great admiration for Nasser as one of the protagonists, together with Chou En-lai, Nehru and Tito, who laid the basis of the policy of non-alignment in Bandung (1957). These two factors, my ignorance of my own country and my admiration for the developments in foreign policy, prevented me from seeing why the political experience acquired through the nationalist movement showed no resistance to an enterprise which clearly aimed at the restoration of an absolute government. It was only after many years during which I was always a frequent visitor to Egypt and even lived there at various periods both during Nasser's life and after, that I could understand the reason for this lack of resistance. Though when I did finally understand what had happened, I was surprised that I hadn't worked it out earlier. Indeed, the failure to resist the imposition of an absolute ruler was evidence that the set of political concepts introduced by the British had made no impact except among the university and high school students and graduates living in the big, more or less cosmopolitan towns. For the vast bulk of the population – that is, the peasants – were as removed from these modes of thought as they had always been from the passage of time, simply waiting for the saviour whom they believed they would find in the man who preached unity against multiplicity. However, by the time of the 1967 defeat, my political experience as an Egyptian citizen had prepared me to find the reasons for that defeat in the nature of our institutions, without any of the standard lame excuses which blamed everything on 'colonialism'.

It was our situation which led me to a sixteenth-century European writer, but I can't say that la Boétie gave a satisfactory answer to the question of why people were so willing to welcome servitude under a single individual. However, translating him gave me the opportunity to write an introduction to his text, in which I tried to explain the reasons why European civilisations had surpassed other civilisations, particularly those Islamic civilisations nearest to, and thus most competitive with, Europe.

The decisive factor, I explained, was the increase in inventions related to means of production and the accumulation of capital that went along with the expansion of trade. It was improvements in the art of navigation, which allowed for the discovery of America, and which also made it possible for ships to round the Cape of Good Hope (which amounted to encircling the unsuspecting Islamic societies), thus linking the world from one end to the other by the sea. The expansion of trade, more particularly, led to the creation of guilds as moral entities which persist over time, in contrast to generations made up of individuals, who pass away. Indeed, these guilds were organised on the basis of representatives elected from among their members. With this emergence of the *idea of representation*, parliament's influence increased and the governed classes were able to voice their opinions to, and sometimes to impose their demands on, kings. Moreover, a new class was born, the intellectual class, which played a very different role in European societies from the role they played in Islamic societies. This led to the creation of universities in Italy, England and France. All these events coincided with the creation of nation states under the control of kings and with conflicts not only between king and king, but also between king and Church.

Before its twelfth-century renaissance, Europe had been formed into a society united under the rule of the 'papal prince'. It was thus the Church that was in charge of defending Europe's frontiers, launching its crusades, resolving its economic and health issues – especially fighting epidemics – as well as promoting education – especially religious teaching. This unity implied a political philosophy that came down to two propositions, or rather to two metaphors. The first metaphor compares society to a body whose legs (i.e. craftsmen and peasants) are on earth, and whose head (i.e. the pope) is in the sky. The second metaphor compares society to the family. Just as the family has an unquestionable head, the father, so society has an unquestionable head, the ruler.[4] Europe's awakening was its departure from this idea of unity, which had been sustained by the metaphor of the body, towards admitting the reality of multiplicity and struggles between states and nations as well as struggles between social classes. Voluntary servitude has its roots in an attachment to the figure of the ideal father, who is the factor that keeps infantilising the people, perpetuating a state of dependency to such an extent that the crueller the ruler, the more his subjects may mourn his loss.

The fact that Europe was the land of Christendom with the pope at its head doesn't, however, mean that the government of the One is necessarily a theocracy. The fact is that the rulers who have brought the most disastrous defeats on their peoples, whether in the West or in the Third World, have been secular. Government is one thing and religion is another. Thus any demand to put both powers, the temporal and the spiritual, into one hand, is misguided, because, whatever the doctrine advocated by the One may be, he will remain a human creature, and Acton's verdict will apply to him: 'Power corrupts, and absolute power corrupts absolutely'. Moreover, being made from human stuff, a monarch is liable to commit errors beyond remedy, since all power lies exclusively in his hands.

But the crucial question is, why is the monarch necessary?

Every human society needs to believe in a transcendental truth, free of any contamination by falsehood or error; a truth where the members of this society meet, and upon which they all agree, and which thus represents for them the ultimate criterion to which they refer when a choice must be made between what should and what should not be done. Indeed, it's the only guarantee of the existence of an eternal order, without which it would be impossible to act today in anticipation of tomorrow. We know that the Greek gods were unscrupulous, deceitful beings, who would break any promise, and betray any alliance; in short, they represented desires rather than ideals. It is therefore no wonder that the Greeks placed truth within nature itself, as realised in the uniform movement of the stars, which always return to the same place, in accordance with the perfection of Aristotle's Prime Mover. In our time, we know that one of the main consequences of quantum theory was to throw doubt on mechanical determinism, but that Einstein refused this conclusion, expressing his refusal in his famous formula: 'Subtle is the Lord, but malicious He is not'.[5] The importance of Einstein's statement is that it reminds us that, after the extinction of polytheism and the advent of monotheism, truth was placed in God himself. One of the best proofs of this is Descartes's conception of eternal truths as a creation of God's will. What are the conclusions that can be drawn from all this?

The first conclusion is that modern dictators always govern in the name of some higher truth, of which they claim to be the representatives and from which they draw their legitimacy. That's why they are keen to hide their most monstrous crimes, especially genocide: because, however complacent the people, it will still be difficult to reconcile such crimes with any pretension to truth.

The second conclusion is that, in spite of the hatred they engender, monotheistic religions still constitute the solid basis of life in our societies and will continue to do so as long as religion is considered to be the locus of ultimate truths which escape both science and philosophy. As long as this situation continues, and as long as there is no new body of dogma which demands universal assent, as Marxism-Leninism did, monotheism will thus continue to be an essential reference for social life.

The third conclusion is that if the will to govern in the name of religion constitutes a fallacy – and sometimes a fraud – fighting religion is a sign of blindness whose cost the former Soviet Union paid through its collapse.

From this point of view, we can say that the Founding Fathers, who wrote the Constitution of the United States, were wiser. The First Amendment, ratified in December 1791, stipulates that Congress shall make no law concerning religious creeds or prohibiting the free exercise thereof, or abridging the freedom of speech or of the press, or the right of the people to assemble peacefully and to petition the government for redress of grievances. Indeed, the only time this government interfered in a religious matter was in 1800, when one sect (the Mormons) declared that marrying more than one woman was a religious duty for men. Then the Supreme Court did interfere, and judged that the above-mentioned sect must abide by federal law that bans polygamy – a judgement that merely reflected custom.

Here I refer back to la Boétie's question: How can one man force millions of people to submit to oppressive and humiliating tyranny? If we recall what was said previously, that servitude has its roots in an unconditional attachment to a 'unity' incarnated in the body's integrity (to the point of refusing difference as being a threat to life), as well as in the no less passionate attachment to the figure of the ideal father who transcends human limits, or, to put it in St Anselm's words, who is so great that we can't conceive anything greater, then la Boétie's question would be better inverted: How did it happen that, instead of assenting to the quasi natural division between the ruler and the ruled, some societies got the idea that the ruler should answer for his actions to the ruled? If we admit that this idea of the responsibility of those who govern to the governed is the core of democracy, the question becomes: How could a democratic regime ever come into being? As far as Europe was concerned, the question wasn't about its dominance but about its road to democracy.

Far from being the political system that best suits the spontaneous tendencies that make for social life, democracy, as a method of government, was a complete novelty when it first came into being in Athens, where it flourished between the sixth and fifth centuries BC. Democracy showed up again in the United States, at the end of the eighteenth century, and in Europe in the nineteenth century. It isn't by chance that, in his *Suppliant Women*, Aeschylus, who surely knew what he was talking about, presents an opposition between the decrees of the pharaoh and the decisions of free people as being between the written and the spoken word. The Danaids, we remember, had fled from Egypt to Argos, seeking protection. A herald asked in the name of the Egyptians that they be given back. The king of Argos, who had refused to take any decision before 'communicating the facts to all the Argians', answered him in these terms:

> By their own will, in kindliness of heart,
> With fair words, win these maidens to depart,
> And none shall check you ... But one oath all through
> My people hath prevailed, and standeth true,
> Never these suppliant maidens to betray;

And fast with nails of iron that oath shall stay.
It is not writ in wax, not shut between
A book's dim pages, sealed and unseen,
'Tis a clear word, outspoken to the light,
From a free tongue.

Go, get thee from my sight!'[6]

Indeed it was my recognition of the fact that in ancient Greece the status and function of writing were completely different from those that were assigned to it in ancient Egypt in particular and the Middle East in general that allowed me to answer the question that I had first posed to la Boétie. The full explanation of this difference is the subject of chapter 6, but I will here draw the reader's attention to a few points.

First of all, kings of the ancient states, either on the banks of the Nile or in Mesopotamia, were always keen to keep a separation between the language that was used in writing administrative and state documents, literature, medicine, magic, arithmetic, religion, et cetera, and everyday spoken language. And they were just as keen to ascribe to the first a sacred character, attributed either to a supposed divine origin or to having been the language of the ancestors. The mother tongue, on the contrary, was scorned as a plebeian idiom, unfit for the expression of lofty ideas, profound significations and elevated feelings, whose appropriate place was only inside the brains of the educated. In a word, the ancient monarchs (who at least had the excuse of being empire builders) behaved toward their subjects just like colonial powers. The coloniser, as soon as he conquers a foreign country, begins by despising the language of the natives so that the natives may despise themselves and refrain from thinking about a freedom that they don't deserve and that doesn't suit them.

Earlier I alluded to the people's tendency toward dependency, if not toward servitude. But in so far as this tendency originates in the relation to a chief taken as a model, it is also in the nature of this same relation to generate envy of the chief's autonomy and freedom if not of his supremacy. Monarchs make peoples in their own image. We know the means they use to fight this tendency: they purchase consciences, spread fear and, most important, forbid any assembly or association that might enable the people to build some solidarity in order to defend their rights. People were assembled, but merely to build pyramids, tombs, temples, palaces, statues and so forth, – they were never allowed to associate for the realisation of a common goal of their own choice. Having no such culture of cooperation, it's all the easier for the monarch, in cases where his injustice, incompetence or hubris leads his people to take to the streets, to crush their demonstrations and arrest their leaders, who quite often just 'disappear'. Demonstrations of resistance may reoccur, but they never throw off the regime. At most, they may encourage a coup d'état. But all of this is part of the politics that aims to keep the subjects under the yoke of the monarch. What is even more pernicious, however, is a politics, to borrow la Boétie's words, that makes the subjects 'forget the very idea of liberty', or remember it, if they ever do, only with sorrowful resignation. Wherein lies this kind of politics? This was la Boétie's main question, to which he never found an answer, perhaps because he hadn't lived in the Middle East.

This politics consisted in banning the mother tongue from schools. Only a language that drew its prestige from being either dead or foreign had the right to be taught in schools. The young then grow up with love for this 'grammatical language', as Dante calls it, so that if they ever turn to writing, their pens become the prison which separates them from their compatriots as well as from the rich resources of their mother tongue. In other words, just as corruption under the monarch's rule does not amount to some reprehensible act of corruption, but simply constitutes a dimension inscribed in the nature of this regime, and just as repression constitutes another intrinsic dimension, so does this politics of writing constitute an undeclared and massive censorship that undermines all thought among the subjects.

It is often thought and said that Arabic is one language, but in fact the distance between classical Arabic and the Arabic of Egypt, the Gulf States and North Africa is analogous to the relation between Latin and the Romance languages Italian, Spanish and French. The failure, or rather the refusal, to acknowledge these differences is the refusal to allow the uneducated a full say in their future. Awareness of the devastating effects of this 'policy of mystification' led me to write, not in 'grammatical Arabic', the language of the elite, but in the vernacular, because this politics of writing persists today, even though you can count all the great living Arabic writers on the fingers of one hand. Ask any current monarch, whether a king, a raïs, a caliph or a sheikh, immediately to publish the amendments to the American Constitution. You will have no difficulty getting his agreement. First, out of a mixture of hypocrisy and ignorance he probably believes that 'there isn't anything new in this, we have it all at home'! Second, he knows his subjects aren't going to believe it anyway, and that even if they did, the words wouldn't stick, because they would be wondering: 'What sort of chief is it who would submit to being questioned and judged by his subjects?'[7] But ask that same monarch to promulgate the study of the mother tongue's grammar in schools, as well as the study of some admirable texts written in the vernacular by authors such as Baïram Al-Tunsi, Fouad Haddad, Salah Jahin, Al-Abnoudi ... he will surely refuse.[8] And most of the elite will share his refusal, and probably the people would too, out of the natural reverence for the order of the 'sacred'. The monarch will refuse because he senses, even if he doesn't actually know, that honouring this request would leave the door open to a discovery that may threaten his domination, a discovery that transforms the people's awareness of its lost liberty and its resignation, from being barely an individual knowledge (even though shared by the many) into an objective truth, put under its eyes in written form, and thus a stimulus to action rather than a matter for jokes.

I don't think the reader needs to be warned that my argument isn't advanced from a Marxist point of view, as some friends have suggested. On the contrary, I would say it's based on considerations Marxism doesn't take into account. What is at stake here isn't class struggle. Class struggle exists and always will, and to its credit democracy tries to attenuate it, while the former Soviet Union wanted to abolish it. But here we are dealing with a different question, which concerns two trends of human thought. The first prefers unity to the point of denying difference, and when reality belies this unity, there is no means of dealing with it other than by calling for the death of those 'outsiders' (*khawaredj*). The result is that the alleged unity remains a mere desire, or a libidinal aspiration, which has no more reality than the petty songs with which the regime tries to drug the people. If this were not true, we wouldn't have witnessed the shameful attitude of the Arab governments and the helplessness of the Arab nations regarding the Palestinian tragedy: Arab rulers preferred, as usual, to keep their thrones, while their subjects preferred, in the end, simply to avoid the oppressive violence of their rulers. The second trend acknowledges difference and endeavours, through negotiations, to reach an agreement that even armed lies could never achieve.

In short, the matter can be summarised in a Zen maxim: As long as we are silent, we are one; if we speak, we are two.

It's up to our writers to choose.

Notes

1   Mohammad A. 'Inan, *Islamic Egypt* (1933, Cairo), ch. 2.
2   Ibid.

3   The word *Khalifa* means successor; considered as 'the successor of the prophet' (a contradiction in terms since Mohammed was the *last* prophet); the *Khalifa* is just as much the representative of God on earth. This claim of the *Khalifa* to represent what Mohammed represented is, strictly speaking, blasphemous.

4   The Arabic word that corresponds to 'responsible' means literally *questionable*. The structure of political power in the Middle East may thus be summarised in the conundrum: the questionable is unquestionable!

5   Cf. Abraham Pais, *Subtle is the Lord . . . The science and life of Albert Einstein* (Oxford: Oxford University Press, 1982).

6   Aeschylus, *Suppliant Women*, ll.940–50. Verse translation by Gilbert Murray (London: George Allen and Unwin, 1930). Emphasis added.

7   In order to justify the interdiction of a work of fiction considered as 'immoral', we recently heard a minister shamelessly declare that he was responsible for the education of the people and for the protection of their morals. And no one found anything wrong with his blunt assertion, as if it were perfectly natural that ministers educate people and defend traditions. Who else?

8   Unfortunately these writers are not translated. Mrs Nihad Salem made a splendid English translation of some of Salah Jahin's work, notably his long poem *'agabi*, but as far as I know this translation has never been published outside Egypt.

1

Components of Western Dominance

It was in the sixteenth century, the century of Etienne de la Boétie, that Europe began that expansion which was to culminate in its current state of wealth and dominance. This expansion was not, as has often been thought, a sudden move from the 'darkness of the Middle Ages' to the light,[1] but the outcome of the remarkable achievements which took place between the tenth and the thirteenth centuries. Many processes, such as the grinding of grain, the sifting of flour, the pressing of fabrics, the tanning of leather, were improved by better exploitation of the energies generated by water, wind, high and low tides. Military technology also improved, but, perhaps more important, the advances in the extraction of metals (silver, tin and iron) made it possible to create ploughs capable of digging deep into the heavy, humid European soil. So striking were the improvements in stone carving that between the eleventh and the thirteenth centuries France extracted more stone from its soil than did ancient Egypt at any epoch of its long history, and one can grasp the significance of this comparison if one remembers that the biggest pyramid alone required 2,500,000 cubic metres of stone. Developments in engineering – the digging of tunnels through the mountains as well as the establishment of canals, dams and reservoirs – enabled the important trade centres of the Mediterranean Sea to be linked to those of the North Sea, with the subsequent growth of trade exhibitions and markets. The use of automated hammers and air pumps to increase furnace temperatures grew to the point when London was the first to complain of pollution in the late 1280s. The extension of cultivated land and the changes in agricultural methods led to an increase in agricultural production, particularly of wheat. Indeed, agriculture became such a focus of interest that books were written about it and some monasteries devoted land to model farms. There was improvement in the breeding of both cattle and sheep. The arts of navigation improved, above all with the development of the compass. Ships could now cross the seas instead of hugging the coast. The drawing of accurate maps, the simplification of trigonometry tables, the construction of new types of ships to carry larger loads at faster speeds, the creation of rudders to set precise courses. All these and many other innovations made it possible both to reach India by the Cape of Good Hope and to discover the New World. Perhaps most important of all is the arrival of a machine whose precision is a model for all others and which produces this wonderful thing without which it is impossible either to calculate energy, or to impose production standards to calculate wages: measured time. The invention of the clock changed social relationships not only between the different classes but also within the same class. For example, bricklayers became more capable than other workers of threatening to go on strike because their wages could not be calculated on the number of pieces produced per hour. The clock affected the whole of society, which moved from a mode of being in which time was inseparable from worship, when people knew the appointed hour by the crow of the cock at dawn and by the church bells ringing at sunset prior to darkness. It was as if it were impossible to refer to time without referring to God and Nature. Clocks ushered in a new era, when time was not related to prayers and to the motion of the stars – dawn, morning, noon, afternoon, sunset, then evening – but was divided into equal units by the chimes of the clocks erected in public squares by order of the state – whether this state was a city like Genoa in AD 1353 or a kingdom like France, where the clock on the Seine's bank, known to this very day as 'Le quai de l'horloge' (the dock of the clock), has rung regularly since AD 1370. Even the Church, in the West, had to accept the clock's hands on its towers after its initial refusal, though the Eastern Church persisted in its refusal. However, if the Western Church finally accepted that time would be submitted to bourgeois interests rather than to eternity's requirements, it was because a new man had appeared in the West, a man for whom time was money.

Indeed, the aforementioned increase in production led to an increase in the population; that is, of both consumers and workers. Moreover, the appearance of Islam did not – contrary to a once prevalent opinion – lead to the separation of East and West. On the contrary, the great urban centres of the East represented a vast domain of consumption without which the resurrection of Western trade would have been impossible. There is no doubt that the merchants in Venice and other Italian Mediterranean coastal cities earned most of their wealth from trade with the Greco-Muslim world from Byzantium to Alexandria. There is also no doubt that they adopted the outlook and the methods from their predecessors, the Byzantine and Arab merchants. These new merchants deserve all the credit for developing and enriching their cities so that, like Venice, they could become genuine states. They also introduced or, better, adopted revolutionary innovations in the domains of accounting, money exchange, insurance, credit and all forms of contracts. They had such a wide geographical and economic vision, and invested such huge amounts of money, that their emergence may well be considered as the emergence of a whole new class. A class that both Church and aristocracy had to take into consideration.

The Church's first response to these men of money could be summarised in the following motto: 'Merchants do not gain God's blessing – or only with difficulty.' However, after two centuries of the expansion of trade and the creation of new crafts in the cities, which extended the domain of work beyond agriculture, the Church included the merchants on the list of workers to whom God refers in Genesis: 'Thou shalt earn your living by the sweat of your brow.' Nevertheless, it continued to condemn usury, which was considered, as Thomas Aquinas put it in the thirteenth century, as 'selling something that has no existence'. The Church's sermons continued to warn usurers and money-changers that 'the money they got from usury would be balanced by the wood that would burn them in hell'. However, who would give to the poor if not the rich? Is not charity a way of laundering profits into holiness? Merchants should be allowed to give to the Church and firstly to those who have foresworn all wealth: the Franciscans. The money can not only build churches but employ the greatest artists of the century to make those churches the monuments to the glory of God that one finds on the streets of Florence and Siena. Does not God allow for profit? Does not each business imply risk? Does not the outcome of each risk depend on the will of God? This was the theology of the Tuscan businessmen; it was best expressed by Saint Bernard, who stipulated that profits gained from investments were justified because they contributed to the good order of Christian society. After all, while it is true that men do not live by bread alone, it is also true that bread is a large part of their diet, and our businessmen, in a praiseworthy endeavour to ease their consciences, did not forget to give the Church the money it desperately needed in its struggle against the princes. Nor did they forget to buy their shares in heaven by stating in their wills that portions of their inheritance should be allocated to the clergy for their charitable work.

If it was easy for businessmen to satisfy the Church and perhaps (at least for a few of them) their consciences by taking doomsday into account, their relations with the nobility were a combination of competition and merger. The competition led to an easy change of status in cities like Florence where many members of the aristocratic families worked in trade because of the profits it offered and because of the failings of the feudal economy. As for merger, it could be witnessed in cities like Genoa or Venice, where the rural nobility flowed into the growing cities; together with the rich merchants, they composed a new aristocracy – a state of affairs which found its best expression in the Venetian phrase: 'The doges are merchants, and merchants are the princes of the sea.' Even in the old cities, where merchants constituted a middle class and were thus snubbed by the nobles as part of the 'people', a harmonious relationship replaced the old fight between the new class and the old aristocracy – a fight which had usually been based on the merchants' refusal of the outrageous taxes the nobles imposed on them every time they crossed their lands or rivers.

The main reason for this change in the relations between merchant and aristocrat was that the merchants were less frightened of the aristocracy than they were of the city workers and craftsmen whose potential class solidarity threatened the merchants' hegemony over international trade and, consequently, their political power. Moreover, it was no longer difficult for merchants to cross the boundaries that separated them from the aristocracy, by contracting marriages with them, buying their lands or imitating their lavish lifestyle. This was the situation in the new cities which they ruled. But in the lands ruled by kings (such as France and England), the merchants did not have such power. They learned from their own experience and even more from others (especially the peasants) that whoever chooses to rebel by force is killed by force.

However, this did not mean that they were not politically influential. Kings and princes had to take their advice on every crucial financial or economic matter regarding both peace and war. Whether in capitals or provinces, merchants were interested in taking part in government decision-making not only to have their own opinions heard but also to hear at first hand the views of those among the participants who were the king's representatives, if not the king himself. This participation was more important for the merchants than acquiring state jobs, although they did not refrain from buying such jobs for their sons and family members, especially, in France, the key position of tax collector. The merchants' expertise and broad political knowledge of the international scene led kings to nominate them as counsellors, diplomats, ministers of finance, and so forth. Most importantly, the kings and princes had to resort to banks for loans to finance their endless wars. This gave the lenders the opportunity to obtain important rights by means of warranties (such as obtaining a certain percentage of the mining production), and concessions (such as the right to rule over occupied territories in Palestine and Syria during the Crusades), in addition to civil and military positions.

These merchants formed, in the true meaning of the word, a new class, whose self-consciousness was crystallised in the corporations that were created in different cities and countries, and which represented their different activities (meat or textile trade, import or export, et cetera) in order to defend their interests. At the other end of the social spectrum, other corporations were similarly created on a professional basis: workers of the same craft joined together to regulate working conditions, the supply of raw materials, the sale of goods and the setting of production standards. Once these matters had been agreed in the formation of a guild, members had to respect the authority of the guild. These corporations and guilds, formed in the Middle Ages, are not related to any institution known in Roman law; no one knows precisely how they were created. If Machiavelli's dictum is right – that class struggle is the key to social progress – then it would not be an exaggeration to assert that the emergence of these guilds was one of the factors that led to the progress of the West.

One of the necessary conditions of these new entities was the existence of the cities within which they functioned. These cities were either totally independent (Venice, Genoa) or had recognised legal privileges (London, Paris) – conditions notably lacking both in China and in the Middle East. These new unions were named 'corporations' (from the Latin *corpus*, a body)[2] because, as a body, they were composed of different members united by an invisible or 'fictitious' force that transformed them into a legal entity, with its own rights, obligations, accounts, seals and emblems. It is therefore no wonder that jurists and philosophers gave these institutions a great deal of attention, which affected political philosophy and particularly thinking about the state. To comprehend the originality of Renaissance political philosophy it is necessary to grasp the impact of these new institutions on political thought.

Political theories in the Middle Ages were based on the concept of the whole. They perceived the universe as a whole and every being, whether a multiplicity (such as a regiment or a corporation) or an individual substance (such as Alexander or his horse), was seen both as a part and as a whole. The relationship of part to whole was understood within Aristotelian notions of causality for which the final ordered state of the universe was the most powerful cause working in the apparently disordered present. This doctrine of final causes meant that each part was determined by the teleological cause of the whole, while the whole enjoyed its own teleological cause. The medieval conception of society followed from this premise. Every human society was a part of the whole that owed its existence to God, and every earthly society was a member of the kingdom of God that included both heaven and earth. As to the principle which governed the essence of the universe and its constitution, it was unity, because God is one and his will is one. But then came the question: how did it happen that human society was split into two systems, the temporal and the spiritual? All medieval political theorists admitted the existence of a higher entity wherein unity was accomplished; but how?

It is obvious that we are dealing here with what political philosophy calls the question of sovereignty, the question of the authority which is above all others. If that authority is dual, then the government is split and civil war casts its shadow. However, we shall see that what was called the fight between the temporal and the spiritual authorities was in fact a constant fight between two powers each of which considered itself to be both temporal and spiritual. For the spiritual power, the Church, religion *was* the government; for the temporal power, the State, religion was the support of the government. The Church's dogma was that if one state on earth were possible that would include all humanity, it would be the Church established by God Himself. This did not mean that the Church refused the principle of separation between the two authorities, but it considered this separation as an expression of God's law, which forbade those who carried the spiritual authority as representatives of Christ from carrying the sword. God gave two swords, the spiritual and the temporal, to Peter and through him to the pope, who keeps the first and gives the second. However, giving the second means, not a capitalist sale, but rather a feudal investiture which allows the recipient its use. The emperor is nothing but the pope's first knight, and the oath he takes in front of the pope when he is crowned is the perfect example of the pledge the knight makes to serve his lord. It is therefore the pope's right, or rather his obligation, to remove the *imperium* from someone who proves to be incompetent or corrupt and hand it to someone better.

The opponents of this dogma had some difficulty in deducing the sovereignty of the temporal authority from the principle of God's unity, although the memory of the centuries after Constantine, when the Church was more or less submitted to the emperor, was still vivid. However, some philosophers, such as William of Ockham and Marsilius of Padua, dared to doubt the necessity of a state including all humanity and led by one head. Were it realised, such a state, they said, would absorb the Church itself: the real principle of unity on earth can only be in the composition of two separate orders. Medieval philosophers were thus divided between supporters and opponents of the sovereignty of the spiritual authority. However, they all subscribed to the idea of human society as a body whose perfection is achieved in its celestial head. Although it clearly indicates the importance of the image of the body in human thought, this idea had some valuable consequences.

The general idea of human society as a whole was soon applied to every particular society: every society is a permanent political body in opposition to the mortal body, an invisible body in opposition to the visible. From this follows the idea of the part as an organ that should be sacrificed in case of conflict between its interests and those of the whole, though such a sacrifice represents a damage to the organism which should be avoided as far as possible. Then, from the idea of the organism that includes both similar and dissimilar parts, we move to differences in status, position and function. It is this thinking which conceives of society as being composed of individuals who are not equal units, but members of different and distinct classes. Similarly, with the differences between the functions and their subordination to a first mover that initiates and guides their activity, the question arises of whether it is Emperor or Pope who fulfils this function. For some authors the metaphor of the body was fallacious, for however numerous the resemblances between the political body and the natural body, they do not erase the differences. These authors, of whom the most important was Marsilius of Padua, affirmed that although God had created the Church directly (a dogma which nobody thought of denying), yet he gave men the liberty to create the state directed by the model of organisation provided by nature. This discourse, as sound as it could be (within the limits of the concepts and mental categories that governed it and whose domination we may still witness in Egypt right up to the present), could not, however, lead to a satisfactory conclusion as long as it lacked a legal framework. What was vital here was the use that these philosophers made of the interaction between the new model of the corporation and Roman law.

If we acknowledge that God is the sole ruler of the universe and that He is the source of every power, then we must conclude that any power on earth, whether spiritual or temporal, represents a small model of the divine power. This was the common belief in the Middle Ages. Yet this belief was never immune from disputation, thanks to the knowledge the authors had of the writings of classical antiquity. The assertion that monarchy was better than any other political system could be put into question thanks to Aristotle's comparison of different political systems and constitutions. It was true that both religious arguments and the German conception of the 'Lord' with his train of knights and his dominion over his land and his serfs tended to elevate the king's position above the society he headed, like God, above the universe – indeed, gave the king a certain divine status as God's representative on earth. Yet this elevation of the king's person was never fully divorced throughout the Middle Ages from the contrary view: that the relation between the king and his subjects consists in mutual rights and obligations between the two parties out of whose union the organic whole is composed. Lordship has never been an absolute right but begins with an obligation. Its divine character only makes it more abiding since it transforms it into a 'commitment': kings are made for the people not the people for the kings. All this was summarised in sovereignty being linked not to the person of the king but to his *office*, the two terms being explicitly distinguished. The way was thus paved for the emergence of the idea of the people's sovereignty through the encounter of the theory of Roman law with the fact of the new medieval corporations.

One of the Church's teachings was that, prior to sin, humanity knew a happy time when people lived according to the laws of God and nature, when they enjoyed wealth, freedom and equality. This dogma was meant to consolidate the Church's position. But its opponents saw in it a proof that the emergence of the rulers was by a decision the people took after the emergence of sin: a contracted subjection similar to the previously mentioned commitment. This was not meant as a denial of kingship's divine origin and right. After all, the people were only a tool in the hands of God, and it was His will to have them choose rulers. This opinion prevailed thanks to the following quotation from Justinian's *Institutes*: 'A pronouncement of the emperor [in addition to the Senate's decrees] also has legislative force because, by the Regal Act relating to his sovereign power, the people conferred on him its whole sovereignty and authority.'[3] The question was therefore the following. Was this voluntary subjection an irrevocable once and for all act that transferred all power from the people, or did the people retain the essence of political power (*imperium*)? Marsilius of Padua introduced a theory applicable to all systems of government, stating that, as long as the ruler is part of the whole, as long as the part is less important than the whole even if it is the main part, and as long as voluntary subjection is itself a legislative act, then the people is the first legislator and the ruler has to abide by the law in his legislative acts since he is only the tool through which the collectivity or the corporation manages to run its affairs. Nicholas of Cusa added that both legislation and administration are based on the election that expresses the will of the whole and in virtue of which the person of the ruler becomes a public common figure. He therefore cannot stand as the father in relation to the individual members unless he acknowledges his debt as an offshoot of the whole.

Aside from the previously mentioned distinction between the person and the office, these theories implied a view of the One, whether he was the emperor or the pope, that put him on the same level as anyone who headed a corporation or guild. The Middle Ages thus owed to the corporations the idea of a state endowed with representative or parliamentary institutions: the emperor is not the empire, but his position represents both the empire as a whole and the citizen as a part. The same interpretation or way of thinking can be applied to the notion of the people's right. This refers not to the personal rights of individuals but to the public right enjoyed by a council formed legally in conformity with the principle also borrowed from the corporations, according to which the majority represents the whole. More explicitly, the representative council acts on behalf of all those whom it represents, so that its decisions may have the same legal force as those taken by a council that would include all the citizens, if it were possible to form such a council. These representatives or deputies exercise their authority as individuals, and their council has rights and obligations, not because it is constituted by them as individuals, but because it is (another concept derived from corporations) a 'fictitious person' or a legal entity. And just as the Church cannot ban corporations, because a corporation is a permanent 'person' that lasts through the succession of generations and such a decision would therefore affect innocent generations, so the king's decisions bind his successors, because the true subject of rights and obligations is not the king as a body but the state inasmuch as it too is a 'fictitious person'.

To sum up, having started from concepts and postulates that would have led to an absolute unification of authority, spiritual as well as temporal, medieval political thought ended up in a dualism that had nothing to do with teleology and final causes and which took many forms: between the king's mortal body and his office, which was permanent; between the One who governs and his subjects; between the people and its representative councils; finally, between the individuals of whom the group is composed and the real subject of rights and obligation who was a 'fictitious person'. This did not mean, however, that medieval thinkers forsook their premises: they kept their 'vertical conception' of the political body that has its summit in God; their views thus remained eminently idealistic, being inseparable from what God's word or its interpretation imposed. We may therefore imagine the shock produced by Machiavelli as he recommended in his sharp style the empirical study of existing political regimes and the nature of peoples instead of the elaboration of fictitious utopianl systems. But before we move to Machiavelli's time, the Renaissance, we have to consider one of the main factors that brought the Renaissance into being: the creation of universities in the Middle Ages.

In addition to the new class of merchants, produced by the development of the means of production between the tenth and the thirteenth centuries, another class appeared whose job was to read, translate, study and teach, and who thus constituted what we might call today the 'intelligentsia', although they called themselves 'philosophers'. They owed their emergence to the West's encounter with the Byzantine and Arab scholars of the East. The encounter was both military, the Crusades, and mercantile, the great Italian trading cities. What it produced was the discovery of the Greek and Latin classics. What these intellectuals, who preferred to read Virgil and Saint Augustine to the book of Ecclesiastes, wanted above all was to study the ancients, of whom they considered themselves to be the heirs. Their position was best expressed by Bernard of Chartres, who headed the school of Chartres in the twelfth century: 'We are like dwarfs on the shoulders of giants, so that we can see more than they, and things at a greater distance, not by virtue of any sharpness of sight on our part, or any physical distinction, but because we are carried high and raised up by their giant size.' They also called themselves the 'moderns' because they realised that 'truth is the daughter of time' as Bernard also said. To measure the novelty of this saying, it is enough to recall the human mind's tendency to tie truth to what is ancient.

Some of these intellectuals did not refrain from criticising the papacy for the alliances it signed with the nouveaux riches. They accused it of turning Christ's name into money, with reference to the words of Pope Gregory VII: 'Christ did not say "My name is tradition" but "My name is truth".' However, if we limit ourselves to the trends which had a constant influence, and if we take the school of Chartres as an example of the scientific centres of the twelfth century, we notice that, although it did not neglect the study of the 'trivium' – that is, grammar, rhetoric and logic – yet it preferred the 'quadrivium' – arithmetic, architecture, music and astronomy – to the study of 'sounds'. This trend, which was enriched by the Arabs and the Greeks and which was characterised by a sense of curiosity, observation and research, was summarised thus by Honorius of Autun (one of the most famous protagonists of this trend): 'Man's exile is ignorance; his home is science.'

This kind of intellectual could only thrive in the cities. The traditionalists, therefore, accused both the intellectuals and the cities. In the city, intellectuals began to consider themselves to be a profession that did not differ from those of other citizens. Their profession was the study and teaching of the 'liberal arts'. If asked what art is, they would answer: 'It is *tecne*.' Art is any steady intellectual activity that the brain may engage in with the aim of producing material and cultural tools. This led to the view that science should not be stored and guarded, it should be spread and promoted: schools are workshops whose products are ideas. The thirteenth century, in which universities were born, was also the century of corporations. Whenever a profession in a city included a large number of people, they organised themselves in order to protect their interests or to create a monopoly. Universities were produced through a number of exchanges: exchanges between teachers and students; exchanges between teachers, students and the other citizens; exchanges between teachers, students and the religious and secular authorities. As they slowly became an important force because of their increasing numbers, a clash was inevitable, in which legislation usually followed events; when the universities won, it was only thanks to their solidarity and tenacity. It is known that the university of Paris, for example, only gained its independence after the bloody events of 1229, during which a number of students were killed. Many of its members went on strike and withdrew to Orleans. As for the scientific and intellectual activities, they attained such a level that written books were no longer a luxury but a teaching tool; thanks to the universities of the thirteenth century, the book was born two centuries before it would live again during the fifteenth-century Renaissance.

With the fourteenth century began the years of misfortunes that lasted for more than a century: epidemics, stagnation and decreasing populations due to starvation, the wasting of resources in endless wars such as the Hundred Years War and the Wars of the Roses. As a consequence, most of the feudal lords preferred to collect their land revenues in cash, not in kind. The gap between the victims and the beneficiaries of the decline increased, especially in the cities, where most of the craftsmen became unemployed and joined the farmers. On the other hand, members of the rich bourgeoisie increased their wealth by exploiting the poor and buying more land, which enabled them to mix more and more with the two other classes that had dominated so far, the nobles and the bishops. These three classes were able to consolidate their situation during the crisis thanks to the political authorities, whose main goal, until the French Revolution, remained the protection of what was called the *ancien régime*. This was also the century which witnessed the emergence of states and nations through the wars between the princes. The rich understood the situation: they understood that it was the prince's time and they hurried to serve him and be part of his entourage in search of wealth, power and glory. In this context, the intellectual of the Middle Ages began to disappear; a new man was to replace him: the *humanist*.

The university authorities did not wait long to freeze the students' grants despite the continuous rise in the cost of living. At the same time they did not forget to increase the price of services: housing, food, books and scientific instruments, examination and graduation fees, et cetera. The best students, who went to the university seeking knowledge rather than positions, left. Furthermore, many university authorities were drawn to the rich, so that they could create faculties to which only the elite could go. Eventually, universities became aristocratic institutions: the humanist was an aristocrat. So much for the universities as institutions – but what were the results on the curriculum?

Fifteenth-century humanists changed the medieval programme of education. They were inspired by Cicero's ideal of the orator as the man in whom perfection is realised thanks to his mastery of such topics as justice, rights, obligations, constitutions, methods of government, in brief of the whole field of practical philosophy. It would not be an exaggeration to say that the aim of their Renaissance was the resurrection of the Ciceronian type. As a consequence, education, in their view, consisted firstly of philological studies, that is, the studies relating to the immortal texts which they adopted as their model and canon. Just as Rome in the first century took the Greek texts as its model, so the Renaissance humanists found theirs first in the great Latin texts, and then – after the fall of Constantinople to the Turks in 1453, and the arrival of the Byzantine scholars in Europe – in the Greek texts. A gap that had no existence in the Middle Ages, between 'men of letters' and 'technicians' originated in the Renaissance. It is to well-read humanists that we owe not only the revival of old languages with all that such a revival entailed – discovering their subtleties; establishing their grammar; reviewing the teaching of grammar, literature and rhetoric – but also the methods they used in the publishing of old scripts with corrections, comparisons, verifications, dates and, most importantly, their historical contexts. To appreciate the impact of such methods, it is enough to recall that the Reformation owed its vigour to the comparison between the Latin translation of the scriptures acknowledged by the Church and the Greek original published by Erasmus for the first time in 1516. These were indeed the methods that paved the way to the incomparable daring of European thought as it called into question the a priori identification of truth with text and as it eventually led to the Enlightenment – without which democracy would never again have seen the light of day in the United States and Europe.[4]

Notes

The first draft of this chapter was the introduction to my translation into classical Arabic of Etienne de la Boétie's *Discourse on Voluntary Servitude*. This translation was published in Cairo in 1991 in an edition so full of mistakes and omissions that it is practically unreadable. Among other things, the publisher simply dropped the bibliography. Other editions appeared in Cairo, Beirut and Morocco which fared no better. In most Arab countries, relations between publishers and authors are not based on written contracts. In working on this chapter, I was indebted to many writers whom I did not cite because I was addressing myself to readers who had no access to their works, but they were included in the bibliography as they are in the list of 'Further Reading' of the current volume.

1   The importance of the first European Renaissance between the tenth and the thirteenth centuries is still not widely enough acknowledged or understood.
2   There is no Arabic equivalent of this term, although it is easy to forge such an equivalent from the triconsonantal *djasad*, meaning 'body'. Translations of *unions* and *syndicates* exist and are used instead.
3   *Justinian's Institutes*, translated with an introduction by Peter Birks and Grant McLeod, with the Latin text of Paul Krenger (London: Duckworth,

1977), 39. Terms relating to political philosophy are poor in the Arabic language in spite of its richness in other fields. There is no exact rendering of even such terms as sovereignty and authority; they are translated by reducing them to words that exist in the Arabic vocabulary, such as *siyadah* or *sultah*, which amounts to abolishing their specificity. A careful translation of the *Institutes* would contribute substantially towards remedying this state of affairs.

4 In his *Radical Enlightment, Philosophy and the Making of Modernity, 1650–1750*, (Oxford: Oxford University Press, 2001), Jonathan I. Israel argues persuasively that the enlightenment of Voltaire, Diderot and Rousseau was preceded by a 'radical enlightenment' in which Spinoza played the pivotal role. According to this line of thought, we may say that it all began with Erasmus.

2

Questions that Have Been Forgotten in our Political Philosophy

I think all Egyptian writers will agree with Dr Fouaad Zakariya's denunciation of our country's current situation as one of unprecedented intellectual backwardness.[1]

This backwardness has two causes. The first is the calamitous degradation of all levels of teaching during the Nasser era, especially in the universities. This was part of a process by which the state monopolised cultural life and established a deadly hegemony by nationalising both the press and book publishing, nationalisations accompanied by the launching of ill-conceived cultural projects that were stillborn. There was, for example, a project to translate 'one thousand books'. The choice of books was going to be made by a 'prestigious committee', but in fact they mainly chose textbooks and the translators, having no personal interest in their task, were more interested in getting paid than doing a good job. The second and no less important reason was that Sadat, fearing opposition from the 'left' (particularly the communists) to his 'offer of peace' to Israel, brought back to life the Islamist movements which had been severely repressed under Nasser, and opened the doors wide to Saudi petro-dollars. The result was that the pavements of Cairo and other cities were piled high with books such as *How to Use the Koran to Cure Illnesses Caused by Djinns*, *The Terrors of the Tomb*, *The Keys to the Unknown*, *Enslavement of Devils*. Books by the most reactionary Islamic thinkers were sold at the lowest of prices.

This intellectual backwardness is most clearly shown in the poverty of our political philosophy – if indeed we have such a philosophy at all. What we do have is a few statements that we keep repeating relentlessly in the hope of turning them into self-evident truths. We do not even dream of questioning ourselves or questioning this 'philosophy' in spite of its substantial resemblance to the dominant philosophy of the European Middle Ages, where it has been studied and criticised for five hundred years. For example, we content ourselves with emphasising the unity of the social community based on history, language and religion, while failing to recognise the divisions due to a multitude of conflicting interests, not least the 'exploitation of man by man'. Another example is the comparison of this unity to a body whose head is in the sky (and, for the faithful, the sky is the Book) and whose feet (i.e. the labourers) are on earth. Moreover, if some measure of mental or inner freedom is attained through assigning ultimate sovereignty to a transcendent entity before which we are all equal, this mental freedom ends in real servitude, in a mode of government where the parts are subjected to the head, that is, the ruler. As to the criteria concerning his legitimacy and the limits of his power, they boil down to an enumeration of some ideal attributes such as wisdom, virtue, due consideration of the *Shoura* (consultative council), and so forth, without setting up any system of checks and balances.

This intellectual backwardness gets worse by the day, because we are dealing with a new kind of colonialism when globalisation destroys the characteristics which every civilisation drew from its own production and in which it could recognise itself. Traditional crafts have vanished, traditional ways of life have changed; food, drink, clothes, housing are no longer the same. Thanks to the media, worship itself has become a kind of spectacle; religion, invaded by television, radio and loudspeakers, has been turned into an electronic event. This phenomenon has deep roots in industrial culture and manifested itself first in Europe. Hegel noted at the beginning of the nineteenth century that this abolition of particularities may deprive a nation of all means of feeling its own existence except through an abstract and lazy emphasis on its identity as it emerges through history, language and, last but not least, through the commandments and prohibitions of its own religion. As Dr Fouaad Zakariya warned, the future is bound under such conditions to be conceived as a return to the glorious past – which amounts in fact to the complete loss of any future. As to the present, it consists either in glorifying our past so that we may heal our wounds, or in picking up some ideas from Western political philosophy without submitting them to the same serious examination to which they are subjected in the West. We are thus divided into two opposite parties.

On the one hand, a party that heads, so to speak, towards the past. Its protagonists are even seen planning for the reconstitution of the Sahaba community[2] that will repeat the conquests of Islam. They forget, for example, that Egypt may be the only country in the world whose military frontiers don't coincide with its political frontiers,[3] and that it may be more worthy of thought to try and find intelligent means of dealing with this situation than to dream of senseless conquests. They also forget to question the meaning of an absolute obedience to the Creator's commandments when such an obedience becomes merely a way of enforcing the commandments of the ruler. They do not refrain from condemning as infidel anyone who does not belong to their circle, thus failing to see that such condemnation oversteps the limits of human justice – since as far as hearts and intentions are concerned, God, by their own admission, is the only judge. As to our traditional scholars (*Ulamaa*) who, let us not forget, are appointed by the head of the state, they think only in terms of commandments and prohibitions, virtues and vices, what is allowed and what is forbidden. Indeed, their obsession with these rules recalls those early Christians who agonised over the questions of whether it was sinful to eat the flesh of animals that had been sacrificed to the pagan gods.[4] One may justifiably ask whether such thinking serves God, or the thinkers' obsessions. More pertinent questions, which would occupy them to better purpose, are: Do God's commandments and prohibitions exhaust His will so that obedience to them guarantees His grace, or is this grace an expression of His free and unfathomable will, which no act can ensure? Is man's hope limited to being found innocent on doomsday, or, given the corruption of the human soul, is it more fundamental to hope for remission and forgiveness? Moreover, can we correctly understand a message that brings previous messages to a conclusion – which Islam claims to be – if we separate the final message from its predecessors? Why did our scholars leave the translation of the Old and New Testaments to the Jesuit fathers who gave us a version which, it is true, is faithful enough to the basic story, but is otherwise shaky, lifeless, inexpressive and unclear? Where can we locate the discrepancy – not only between the commandments and prohibitions, but also between the religious content and biblical stories – which divides the Koran and the two other books which are also believed to be of divine origin? Are these discrepancies to be located in the different historical moments when the messages were revealed and the different communities to which they were addressed? How are we to understand these different periods and different communities? And how can a message claim universality if it is addressed to a particular community?

Multitudes of essays and books dealing with such topics are published every week in Europe and the United States. Both authors and readers consider them a means to attain a more penetrating understanding of religion, its teachings and its place in individual and social life. As to faith, they all behave as if they have fully understood what the Koran repeatedly says, namely that it is a gift that God bestows according to His free will. Consequently, He alone knows those who *truly* have faith and those who don't, and He is the only judge in this matter. Lack of faith never justifies exclusion from civil or political society. Herein lies the strength of contemporary Western nations: no religious sect – which our fundamentalists finally are – can tax the other members of the community with being 'infidel' and go to war against them. A main cause of civil war (as for example, in contemporary Iraq) is thus avoided, and the nation can remain unified in struggles and disagreements with other nations. Whether they serve the temporal power of Mubarak, or whether, as fundamentalists, they claim the temporal power for themselves, our *Ulamaa* behave exactly like the medieval Catholic Church in claiming a monopoly of truth. By insisting that they are the only authorities qualified to interpret the Koran – that is, by excluding others from the field of Truth and denying them the capacity to seek it for themselves – they act like the most dogmatic Catholics. I would even say more arbitrarily and more whimsically than modern Catholicism allows, if we remember that the notion of the infallibility of the pope was forged not to increase his power but to curb it: a pope cannot nullify the decisions of his predecessors, since they were infallible! But an imam, a man considered as a religious authority or as the head of a school, is free to contradict other imams.

The second, so to speak 'secular', party includes those who feel enthusiastic about the 'rights of man', but fail to ask themselves – at least as a hypothesis – whether such an insistence on man's rights is not a function of man's oblivion to his duties. Why should we claim so noisily our right not to be killed or tortured, instead of reaffirming our duty not to kill or torture our neighbour? If we understood that the notion of the rights of man is concerned, not with the relations between individuals, but with the relationship between individuals and their governments, then Western states would almost certainly not be so keen to harp on about states that do not guarantee human rights. For it is the Western states who were the first to rob other nations' rights and to commit the most flagrant acts of injustice both on the individual and collective levels, in their colonialist enterprises. And consider the way in which the Western powers act as though they were the sole legislators on earth, arbitrarily condemning as criminal other people's struggle for liberation or independence.

As for democracy, we are right to argue for it, but if we are arguing seriously we need to think about what the Greek historian Thucydides wrote twenty-five centuries ago: that democracy as a system of government only works for countries like Athens whose military power guarantees control over a number of colonies and thus a certain level of wealth that eases the class struggle. If we want to probe into his remarks, we should ask how democracy can be exported from the West to a country with a different economy and a different class structure. That question entails further questions about the very definition of democracy. Is it mainly based on the multiplicity of parties? What if one party remains endlessly in power to the exclusion of all others? Is it based on the parliament? What if the parliament turns into a closed circle where every member pursues his own interests? – a transformation which one might argue is inevitable once the democratic city state of Athens is replaced by the huge industrial nations of the modern era where Athenian forms of direct democracy are impossible and everything must be decided by universal suffrage. And with the vote comes another set of questions. What is the real relation between the voters and their representative? What is the meaning of this representation? Does the representative replace the voters – if this is what it means – because they merge into him or because he merges into them? Does he speak on their behalf to say what he thinks or what they think? Does this representation comply with the concept of equality that some consider an essential demand of democracy (which leads to referendums on each crucial issue and, economically, to communism)? Or, as the liberals argue, does the essence of democracy lie not in equality, which should not go beyond equality before the law, but in freedom, in which a society allows natural differences to grow freely? The reader may say that in reality most of these questions are academic. Modern democracy is defined by universal suffrage: every individual, whatever his importance or social rank may be, has only one vote, and that vote is exercised on programmes that are presented by parties to the people. Here we tend to content ourselves with vague praise for the people and its will as the source of all power, without taking into consideration the differences of opinion that prevail in the West regarding the definitions of the people (is it the nation, or part of it, and, if so, which part?) and its will (is it a concept of abstract public law or a permanent, autonomous force, beyond a particular result in a vote, referendum or poll?). We equally ignore questions about the relation between state and people, questions such as Hegel's dictum that the people is that part of the state that does not know what it wants, or that sometimes knows what it does not want. It would take too long to discuss here the notion of leadership, for which no one has yet found a satisfactory definition, and its relation with the people. So difficult is this concept that some have been driven to say that 'people' is the collective term a wide variety of leaders make use of in order to create the mirror in which they may contemplate their own glory.

What is more significant is that often we not only admire and utter these notions without really questioning them but, worse, we justify them by assimilating them into the Islamic heritage. We thus identify democracy with the *Shoura*, or consultative council, which is an altogether false identification since *Shoura* is linked to a method of government in which the government acts as trustee for the people, whereas democracy profoundly rejects such a notion of trusteeship in favour of originating power in the people. Equally false is the *rapprochement* between the notions of *public interest* and community, because the first is mainly an administrative concept that supposes the existence of civil society, while the second suggests a spiritual unity and is applied in the first place to those who pray in the mosque: if it refers to another notion it would be that of the imam.

In making these false comparisons, we forget to put the following questions. Have we ever known at any time in our history anything that resembles civil society? Have we not interpreted the saying that Islam is both a temporal and a spiritual power as if it meant the supremacy of the spiritual in all aspects of worldly life, while at the same time we submit it to the authority of a caliph or a sultan – that is, in the last resort, to a political power? Did we not thus make a mess of what was supposed to be a distinction?

The future is unknown. Nobody knows which party it will favour, or whether it will produce something completely unforeseen. As to the present, all we can see is helplessness or impulsive reactions dictated by Western policy and the supremacy of technology over the destiny of human societies. There is no current articulation of ideas that offers us the possibility of changing ourselves so that we may have a historic and not merely geographic existence. This is the task facing intellectuals in our countries, above all those in our universities, both religious or lay, teachers and students alike.

Notes

The first draft of this chapter was published in *Ibdaa* in Cairo in 1991.

1 Dr Fouaad Zakariya was a professor of philosophy at Heliopolis and director of the magazine *Contemporary Thought* in the 1960s. He left Egypt to take up a chair at the University of Kuwait. His theses can be read in articles in *Akhbar Aladab* and *Ibdaa*.
2 The group of men who were the first to join the Prophet and fight beside him. The first caliphs who expanded the Islamic conquests were chosen from this group.
3 According to the Camp David treaty signed by Anwar al-Sadat and Menachem Begin under the auspices of President Jimmy Carter, Egypt is not allowed to deploy its army in Sinai.
4 See Dale B. Martin, *The Corinthian Body* (London: Yale University Press, 1995), 190.

3

Creative Transmission and Stagnant Transmission: Culture and Power

What I would like to show here is the difference between, on the one hand, 'civilisation' considered as a phenomenon that appeared with the creation of the archaic states and empires, and whose duration went hand in hand with a mode of stagnant and monotonous transmission, the same plough labouring the same Egyptian soil for thousands of years; and, on the other hand, 'culture'. I use the term 'culture' to denote what I consider to be a specifically European phenomenon, one that first appeared between 1050 and 1250 bringing with it a new mode of transmission which is the very secret of the power of the West.

One of the famous aphorisms of Lichtenberg, the German eighteenth-century thinker, tells us that 'There exists a species of transcendental ventriloquism by means of which men can be made to believe that something said on earth comes from Heaven.'[1]

Opinions may vary on whether truth is in the last resort an earthly or a heavenly dictum. My thesis is that there is no place on earth for a human society without some reference to heaven.

It is true and self-evident that human speech drafts laws, but it is also true – though it may not be equally obvious – that there are laws drafted by no one's speech and to which all speech is submitted.[2]

Take for example the prohibition of lying. There is no speech that does not presume its own truth as may be attested by the fact that no one would tell a lie without betting on the other's belief that what they say is true. Viewed from this angle, the prohibition of lying may be considered as a reminder of this dimension, which is inscribed in the nature of speech.

As a second example, let us consider the prohibition of murder. We appreciate its meaning if we notice that speech is the only escape route that allows us to break free from the Hegelian dialectic of the master and the slave, with the deadly 'struggle for prestige' that that implies. I refer here to the eloquent description that Claude Lévi-Strauss gives in his *Elementary Structures of Kinship* of the tension that arises between two persons who meet by chance in some restaurant in the south of France and find themselves sitting face to face at the same table. It is not the exchange of wine that eases the tension, as Lévi-Strauss observes.[3] This would have no effect if done in silence.[4] The exchange of wine is merely the celebration of the exchange of speech which is what truly brings peace. The prohibition of murder commands us to have recourse to speech as the condition of coexistence, Heidegger's *Mitsein*.

Moreover, if we take into consideration that the most elementary form of speech is not assertion, as logicians and the great majority of linguists presume, but demand,[5] we shall admit that lack is the mother of speech and that there is no grounding of the talking subject as such without the introduction of an original and indelible lack. And here we come to the function of a third commandment: the prohibition of incest,[6] forbidding the sexual enjoyment of the very person, the mother, who satisfies the other kinds of lack, those that pertain to the biological needs as well as the call for love. The mother feeds and loves, but if there is not something which the child is deprived of, then the child cannot experience desire.

Similarly, if the act of giving did not entail the obligation of giving in return, then that would mean the end not only of exchange, which is, as Marcel Mauss says, the soul of social existence, but of all subjective responsibility.[7] I would say that this obligation is what introduces the perspective of truthfulness in our speech. It is the fact that my speech is always a reply which means that I am always responsible for its truth.

There is no human society that ignores – I do not say respects – these commandments either in written or unwritten form. No society considers any of its members as the author of these commandments, however elevated his rank or his status, because there is no legitimacy unless one is authorised or claims to be authorised by those very commandments. Unlike statutory laws, they are generally attributed to the ancestors, the gods, or to some divine or transcendent being. More precisely, these laws, which underlie the function of language as a social tie and as a means of communication and transmission, induce on the imaginary level the fiction of a transcendent lawgiver.[8] If we consider the ten commandments as stipulating the laws of speech, then we may consider the story of the God of Moses dictating them as representing the closest approximation to what is at stake in the symbolic order.[9] We touch here on the founding priority of belief, namely the belief in the transcendence or thirdness (outside any dual intersubjectivity) of the lawgiver in relation to what is being instituted; it is this exteriority which is the secret of authority. Religion, beyond all ideology, is the last resort, where these commandments find their ultimate ground. It institutes and cements social coexistence by grounding it in the common belief in a transcendent object, which is irreducible to the duality of me and you. Thanks to it, the order of the imaginary becomes instrumental in incarnating the symbolic in human society. If religions are different in spite of this universal function, it is because every religion adds to these four command-ments new ones derived from custom. As a matter of fact, laws of custom are as strong and as imperative as religious laws[10] and are frequently endowed with a sacred or religious character; one need only think of food and drink taboos or of the laws of marriage and inheritance in Islam. Moreover, religion usually specifies the category of those who are allowed to speak to the people in the name of God or of the gods: the elderly, the soothsayers, the prophets, the kings, the priests, and so forth. Every religion also dictates the rituals of worship, especially those of prayers and sacrifices. To put it in a nutshell, just as the universal is only concretised in the particular, so religion cannot be put in the service of the symbolic commandments without serving the group's narcissism.

Some may say that this situation applies to ancient societies and that modern societies are meeting on new ground: science, not religion. However, the upsurge of religious feeling and movements, both in the East and the West, with an intensity unequalled since the Crusades, not to mention the increase in racism, prove this assertion to be highly misleading. Facts show that Malraux was probably right when he said: 'The twenty-first century will be religious or it will not be.' If we look at the past, we note that the very idea of an intrinsic opposition between science and religion is totally wrong. Modern science owes its existence to four men: Copernicus, who was a clergyman, influential in Poland; Kepler, who went to the university of Tübingen to study theology but who had such a conspicuous gift for mathematics that his teachers sent him to teach mathematics and morals at the university of Graz; Newton, who wrote more about theology and the Old Testament than about physics and mathematics. Only Galileo makes us think of a collision with the Church. But Galileo's story is not a simple one.

Galileo was the first man in history to realise fully that there was a certain system of science that had begun to disappear – namely the

Aristotelian system based on the common-sense's view of things as individual substances – and that a new system was about to take its place: mathematical science. That meant transforming the universe into a set of letters and numbers arranged into equations, and by the same token transforming the man of science into a subject that has nothing to do with subjectivity since it is devoid of all psychological or even human attributes; its sole definition, as given by Descartes, lies in thought. Moreover, Galileo improved the quality of the lenses in his telescope, which enabled him to discover the four moons of Jupiter – a discovery which amounted to a visible refutation of the Aristotelian thesis according to which the earth was the only centre around which the other planets rotated. This made it difficult for him to accept the compromise suggested by the Church, which claimed that Copernicus's and Ptolemy's theories were equally valid since each of them merely 'saves the phenomena' – only God knows the truth. Galileo, on the contrary, like Copernicus before him and Newton after him, believed that God's greatest grace was to allow us to know some of the truths He knows. Moreover, Galileo was one of the greatest propagandists ever known, with a unique style in seventeenth-century Italian prose; and the fact that the Medicis protected and generously helped him triggered the Jesuit anger and their subsequent plots against him in a way that reminds us of the tragedy of Robert Oppenheimer, the father of the atomic bomb, during the age of McCarthyism in the United States. In brief, Galileo clashed with Aristotelianism in the first place; his clash with the Church was a consequence. The fact that he reluctantly stood in the court of the Roman Inquisition does not cast doubt on the truthfulness of his belief in the Holy Roman Church. There were many men of great genius in both science and religion in the seventeenth century. It has rightly been called the century of geniuses, of whom Blaise Pascal was pre-eminent.

Even in the present time we know how displeased Einstein was when quantum theory began throwing doubt on the mechanical determinism that had characterised science since it settled under Newton, and how he expressed his irritation in the famous phrase: 'I am convinced that *He* [God] does not play dice.' Indeed, it may be argued that, once discovered, a scientific equation tends to be retroactively objectified as having been there all the time in some infinite mind. The opposition between science and religion is far from being as sharp as its protagonists pretend it to be. This brings us back to the question of the meaning of secularism.[11]

Does secularism mean a completely atheist society? This is an illusion more tenacious than the 'illusion of religion' itself. Communism, although it was itself a kind of faith, paid dearly for embracing this illusion. Religion is the soul of all society and not only of a 'soulless society'.

Does secularism mean the separation between religion and the state? Such a separation between the two powers is indeed possible. But we should not forget that we then witness a set of phenomena that remind us of the Freudian mechanism of repression and the return of the repressed. Otherwise, what would be the meaning of symbols and ceremonies such as coronations, openings of parliament, flags for which citizens die or oaths like the one that the president of the United States takes with his hand on the Bible? Not to mention press conferences: we need only watch any political leader (Chirac, Bush, Blair) on television, in one of these conferences, to see a perfect example of political priesthood. Political ceremonies are indeed a reminder of ritual, in as far as they refer us, that is you and me, to a third or transcendent level, be it that of the divine or, just as sacred, that of values.

To find an unambiguous answer to the question of the meaning of secularism, we have to distinguish between two dimensions of social life.

The first is the horizontal dimension. It consists in the sum of ideas that include technical knowledge such as land surveys, ceramics and city fortifications, as well as social and religious beliefs. In reality, it is often difficult to separate what pertains to knowledge and what pertains to belief, although they are easily distinguished in the mind. One of the best examples of the way in which questions of abstract knowledge are tied up with the complexity of social life is the contribution of Islamic mathematicians, such as Thabit Bin Kura, Al-Khawarizmi and Kashi, in the development of mathematics: they deserve all the credit for transferring the centre of gravity in that science from geometry to algebra. However, this development was most probably due to the complexity of inheritance problems created by the Islamic law, problems that would not have appeared in a society where all the inheritance goes to the eldest son.

The second dimension is the vertical one, by which I mean transmission from one generation to the other. This transmission generally lies in the education that the family undertakes first, followed by religious or state institutions, although the family itself may be considered as an offspring of the state and/or religion since one of them, if not both, is in charge of validating and annulling the marriage contract. Secularism, as I propose to define it, is a complete break with these traditional forms of education and transmission. This break is the culture that I referred to as a purely European phenomenon and which appeared between the middle of the eleventh and thirteenth centuries.

It was in this period that the empire built by Charlemagne, with its claim to be the legitimate heir of the Roman empire, lost power to the nascent monarchical nation states, particularly England and France. These emerging nations were still, however, relatively weak and certainly did not extend over all of Europe. The Church was thus the most important state in the continent, to the extent that some historians talk about a 'papal empire'. It was responsible for defending Europe's borders from the attacks of the Muslims in the south and of Scandinavian tribes in the north. It also launched the Crusades in the south and its missions in the north – in Denmark and the Baltic states, some of which, like Lithuania, had remained pagan until the thirteenth century. It was the state in charge of Europe's international as well as national affairs, such as collecting taxes, mobilising armies and fleets, building cities, bridges, hospitals and churches, and supervising marriage contracts, funerals, heritage distributions and censuses. As for education, needless to say that was solely in the Church's hands. It is true that the separation between the temporal and spiritual powers – based on Christ's saying, 'Render therefore unto Caesar the things which are Caesar's; and unto God the things that are God's'[12] – is one of the Christian principles that was never forgotten. However, another of this religion's teachings is that Jesus gave Peter two powers symbolised by two swords, the religious and the temporal. From which arose the question that echoes down the Middle Ages – who is Peter's successor? The Church thought that both swords belonged to it; the one, spiritual, was, obviously, its inalienable property; the other was for the Church to dispose of as it saw fit, and the emperor that it chose to invest with this power was the Church's servant, though the emperors held that their power came to them not from the papacy but from their own right of succession.

However, what is of more importance to us is that the Crusades had consequences that the Church did not expect. They multiplied the ties between Christendom and the world of Islam and thus enabled the Western Europeans to discover the Greek heritage treasured by the Islamic civilisation in the form of original texts, translations and commentaries – in addition to what they found in Byzantium. A new class developed in the many cities that appeared during this period, a class of men whose only occupation was learning and teaching. These 'brain workers', to give them a name that expresses the way they viewed themselves and the role they played in that ebullient period, became centres around which young people who belonged to the rising bourgeoisie developed and evolved. A new social category composed of them and their disciples appeared in a society where merchants, craftsmen, clergymen and nobles considered themselves not as individuals equal before the law but as social groups each of which had its own rights and privileges. Indeed, the great struggle between Church and Emperor, as well as subordinate struggles which involved kings, nobles and cities, allowed the members of each category of European society to join together in order to defend their interests in associations called corporations. These corporations, as we have already stressed, were the creation of Western European society and had no basis in Roman law. They soon became a power to be reckoned with. The notion of an 'absolute monarch' is not a medieval one; medieval kings consulted councils that included representatives of different groups. It was through following this corporative model that the 'brain workers' joined forces and became a creative power. Together with their students, they formed the universities that took advantage of the fight between the different parties to establish their programmes and syllabuses independently. Each party was generous in offering money because of the increasing influence of the universities on young people, and the universities accepted the money on their own terms; if the would-be donor set unacceptable conditions they would turn to another of the parties in the interminable political struggles.

One example of such a donation and the way that it fed into the development of a university was the right that Frederick Barbarossa granted to the university of Bologna in 1158 to allow foreign students the right of residence. As a consequence, the students, who came with their families, acquired great influence in questions of administration; and interest in theological studies decreased whereas social studies, especially law, became so important that the university enjoyed an international reputation in that field. Matters followed a different course in the university of Paris. In 1219, Pope Honorius III ordered the suppression of civil law studies, probably under pressure from Philip II, king of France, who feared the impact of these studies on the French common law. Instead, Philip offered the university great benefits that made it the Mecca of philosophy and theology students, so that foreign students were more numerous than French students. On the other hand, Oxford University, which had not yet gained the same fame, preserved its traditional method in the teaching of theology and concentrated studies on the explanation of the Holy Scripture. It was not keen to study philosophical problems introduced by Aristotle, Ibn Rushd (Averroes) and Ibn Sina (Avicenna), but it gave their books on nature great attention. No wonder that one of its graduates was Roger Bacon.

These universities, whose appearance had not been foreseen by the Church, were fortresses where thought that was independent of any government, whether temporal or spiritual, could be transmitted. In that sense, I say they were secular institutions. Just as the sixteenth century witnessed the appearance of the humanist inspired by the Ciceronian ideal of the orator, the thirteenth century witnessed this new phenomenon: the replacement of the bishop and the priest by the teacher as a commentator on doctrines and texts, authorised by an independent institution, if not by himself. Indeed, these teachers soon replaced the bishops and other religious figures as creators of doctrines that affected the Church itself. On the other hand, university graduates were the elements that no state could do without in fields such as law, engineering, medicine, art or architecture. States did not create universities in Europe, as was the case in Egypt and many other colonised countries; on the contrary, they thrived alongside them. If it is an overstatement to say man reached adulthood in 1250, it is true that many historians agree that it was then that man started to stand on his own feet and to see the world around him. Without this development, emergence of science and the modern age would not have been possible. How could Copernicus exist without the university of Bologna or Kepler without the university of Tübigen? Galileo would not have existed without the university where he studied and taught, the university of Padua, nor would Newton without Cambridge.

Things took a different course in our part of the world and I do not need to dwell on it long. The Middle East is the cradle of civilisation, where states appeared which, thanks to the art of writing, became empires. However, the natural tendency of the state to enslave other states and its own people, if possible, led these states to make the art of writing serve the state's own aims. They limited the teaching of writing to a certain category of civil servants and kept the people from all contact with it. From this perspective it is significant that a great number of people from the land where writing first appeared are still illiterate. It makes it easier for the state machinery to keep its subjects under state control. This deep fear of the people, a fear deep in the Leviathan of our state and that goes back thousands of years among us, this fear that is 'the most malignant vice of the soul', to quote Bulgakov, has corrupted even the function of the word among us. From a tool for commitment, it became a tool to escape all commitment. One may suspect that the expression 'God willing' (*Insh'Allah*) that we use with every agreement or promise does not emanate from an authentic belief, but aims at avoiding the assumption of a clear-cut responsibility.[13]

I am talking about the state and not about religion. It is true that religion is conservative by nature, but this characteristic is the conservatism of the community's determination to survive, while the state's conservatism is to conserve the power and privileges of those who run the state. To say that the supremacy of the West over the East is due to differences between Christianity and Islam which make Christianity open to argument and Islam a closed monolith is a nonsense which can be refuted with two different examples. First, Islam opened up in some periods to a very serious and fruitful discussion between 'those to whom judgement belongs', *ashab alra'y*, that is the traditionalists, and 'the friends of the new', *ashab alhadith*, that is the modernists. Second, when the emperors of Christianity itself settled in the East, in Byzantium, and acted as the Persian kings did (the kings of kings, as they called themselves), copying the luxury and splendour of their courts – just as the caliphs of the Umayyads and Abbasids did – then Christianity started to decline; with the exception of icons, it left no trace that could be compared to what was left by Islam or Western Christianity.

It would be more accurate to say that Islam was the victim of the nations it invaded, because they themselves were the victims of political regimes and administrative apparatuses whose sole purpose was to ensure the state's domination over all the aspects of life. As a result, we became a nation ready to applaud anyone who, overwhelmed by the madness of megalomania, pretends to be the One who will 'straighten things up'. A nation who waits for the coming saviour will experience nothing but one disappointment after another.

What about culture? If we mean by this term, according to the definition given above, a method of creative transmission, then all we can say is that Egypt – let us limit our talk to this country – is not void of cultured people but is void of culture.

From which we see that our writers' task is not to defend our culture or to predict its future[14] but to create it. It is an impossible task unless they follow the steps of the creator and start from where He started. He told his prophet: 'Read.'[15]

When our writers start manufacturing letters from any material, wood, iron or plastic; when letters are spread in Egypt like sand and when its sons are able to compose from these letters verses of revealed books, poems, songs, popular sayings or whatever may be their inspiration . . .

When our writers start to form schools to teach arts such as drawing, sculpture, poetry, narration, journalism, theatre, et cetera, in addition to the elements of different sciences . . .

When they find the courage to break the barrier of classical Arabic, since, despite our love of it, it binds us, whether we like it or not, to the regime and makes of us an 'elite' group who read one another but who have no communication with the common folk . . .

When they succeed in convincing rich or ambitious Egyptian capitalists to finance their projects . . .[16]

When they are ready to resist the repression that the state will surely exert upon them . . .

Then we may say that a ray of culture has dawned on Egypt and that we have started to stand on our own feet.

This has nothing to do with the slogan 'speak truth to power'. The trouble with this slogan is that it ignores the fact that power will not listen, and that the people already know the truth, as they make clear in their jokes. The aim of writing should be to furnish the materials with which people may articulate a fuller understanding of their situation. At the moment the majority of intellectuals restrict themselves to self-satisfied irony expressed in the classical language which makes them accomplices of the despot. If someone like Adonis uses the classical language to real purpose, it remains a dead letter because of the barrier between the classical and the vernacular language.

Notes

A first draft of this chapter was published in *Ibdaa*, November 1992.

1   Georg Christoph Lichtenberg, *The Waste Books*, trans. R. J. Hollingdale (New York: New York Review Books, 2000), 93.
2   Cf. Moustapha Safouan, *Speech or Death? Language as Social Order: A Psychoanalytic Study*, trans. Martin Thom (Basingstoke: Palgrave Macmillan, 2002).

3 Claude Lévi-Strauss, *The Elementary Structures of Kinship*, rev. edn, trans. James Harle Bell, John Richard Von Sturmer and Rodney Needham (ed.) (Boston: Beacon Press, 1969), 59.

4 Some exchanges take place in silence. A group of strangers come in their boats. They leave gifts or goods on the seashore and return to their boats. The natives venture out to the coast, take the gifts and leave something in exchange. In as far as the whole process is carried out as a dumb show, it is rather a sign of diffidence and leads to no peace.

5 Even assertions imply what Victor Brochard, in his *De l'erreur* (Paris: Felix Alcan, 1926), called 'l'élément volontaire du jugement', that is, the irreducible will that 'lies behind' the union of the subject and the predicate.

6 The prohibition of incest cannot be explained by reference to laws of marriage or exchange. For no such laws could explain why a mother could not introduce her son to sexual intercourse before marriage.

7 See Marcel Mauss, *The Gift: The Form and Reason for Exchange in Archaic Societies*, trans. W. D. Halls (London: Routledge, 1990).

8 I don't need to underline that the conception advocated here has nothing to do with Tönnies's idea of 'A fictitious person [who] can be imagined as *emerging* out of a system of real but solitary persons (human beings)', which merely represents a transposition in the field of what he calls 'civil society' (*Gesellschaft*) of the medieval conception of the corporation as a 'moral entity': Ferdinand Tönnies, *Community and Civil Society*, ed. Jose Harris, trans. Jose Harris and Margaret Hollis (Cambridge: Cambridge University Press, 2001), 185.

9 Cf. Safouan, *Speech or Death?*, ch. 4.

10 For example, polygamy is authorised by Islam. However, the Egyptian Muslim bourgeoisie have an aversion to it. No family would accept the marriage of their daughter to a married man, and no girl would accept it either.

11 The Arabic word *'ilmanyia*, which was used to translate secularism, is derived from *'ilm*, meaning science.

12 Matthew 22:21.

13 One of the most current words in the Egyptian jargon now is the word *taqriban*, meaning 'almost'. You may ask someone if Mr so and so is at his office and get the answer: taqriban!

14 I am referring to a wide literature the best example of which is Taha Hussein's *Mustaqbal al-thaqafa fi misr* (The Future of Culture in Egypt) (Cairo: Matba 'at al-Ma-arifwas Maktabat Masr, 1938). The author argues that culture in Egypt is part and parcel of the 'Mediterranean culture', meaning culture stamped with the Greco-Roman heritage. This is wishful thinking as argument.

15 This is the first word of the revelation Mohammed received from God as narrated in the Koran.

16 We know the part played by philanthropy in spreading American culture: museums, institutes for advanced studies, orchestras, et cetera. It is clear that the millionaire philanthropist has no place in a state that allows no initiative that escapes its control.

4

Peoples and Writers

No logic will overthrow the traditions we have received from out fathers, traditions as old as time, no matter what clever arguments are thought up by the greatest minds.

Euripides, *The Bacchae*[1]

The thesis that the varieties of Arabic languages spoken currently in many different countries represent languages different both from each other and from the *Qureish* Arabic, the language of the Prophet's tribe and in which the Koran was thus revealed, is no novelty. It was already affirmed in the fourteenth century by no less an authority than the great Arabic thinker Ibn Khaldoun in his well known *Introduction*.[2] Nobody has ever explained better than him the difference between knowing a language by birth and oral transmission, and knowing it by study and learning. Study may enable someone to know the structure of a language but the structure itself is not the language. The learner may thus be compared to someone who can say something about the art of sewing without having the ability to sew. In Ibn Khaldoun's terms they has the knowledge of the faculty but not the faculty itself.

I can only agree with him in affirming that the differences between the spoken Arabic – and I am mainly thinking of the idiom spoken in Egypt – and *Qureish* or Koranic Arabic are as significant as those between Italian and Latin. Whatever the semantic and syntactic affinities between Italian and Latin, an Italian speaker has to study Latin in order to understand it.

If we compare spoken Egyptian and classical Arabic we can note that in classical Arabic the predicate usually precedes the subject, whereas in Egyptian the subject precedes the predicate. Moreover, the negative and interrogative particles are not the same and they obey different word-order rules. This is also true for demonstratives. Nouns in classical Arabic decline, but they don't in spoken Egyptian. Phonological differences are no less important. For example, dental fricatives don't exist in spoken Arabic – whether voiced, as in *the*, or unvoiced as *th* in *third* – as well as some other consonants. As for vocabulary, it is true that an enormous quantity of words are common between the two languages. However, most of these have changed through the centuries, some changing the order of letters and some dropping or adding letters. And that's before we start talking about meaning change and neologisms. To all this we must add a substantial number of words that go back to ancient Egyptian. For example, Egyptian peasants still use Coptic names to indicate the months of the year.

Before the Arab conquest there were three languages current in Egypt: Greek, which continued to be the administrative language after the Roman conquest, Latin and Coptic – the native language. As to the Arab conquerors, they were not all from the *Qureish*; many if not most belonged to other tribes which spoke different idioms, so that the Egyptians had to make, you might say, their own cocktail of Arabic, which was not necessarily the same as the *Qureishi* tongue. More of them came to talk *their* Arabic as more of them converted to Islam for a variety of reasons, amongst which one has to note the exemption from the tax each adult Christian male had to pay, the *jizya*. When, in AD 705, Abdelmalek Ibn Marawan issued a decree imposing Arabic as the official administrative language, many Copts had to learn it in order to keep their offices. The distinction between the written and the spoken languages, which had existed in Egypt from the beginning of its history, was thus revived in a new form.

My understanding of the political significance of this divorce between political and demotic Arabic and the key place of writing in the perpetuation of despotism crystallised when I read the work of our great poet Adonis, entitled *The Book*. It is one of the most revolutionary books I've read in Arabic literature. Apart from its provocative title, it lays bare the truth of our political history as having been a series of assassinations in a struggle for power. But it's written in such a high style that it's a difficult text even for the educated, without taking into account the immense majority of illiterate folk. So, it is no wonder that *The Book* has remained a 'dead letter'. I may say that I once heard Adonis declare that he won't ever write except in 'grammatical' Arabic because he prefers writing in a 'dead language'. One may wonder if his choice doesn't also represent his method for dealing with the condition Leo Strauss described in his *Persecution and the Art of Writing*.[3] The authorities are happy to ignore such books because in the unlikely event that they themselves have understood them, they know that their message will only reach a very limited number of people. *The Book* was translated into Spanish and Swedish. A French translation is expected shortly.

It was thus the greatest modern example of classical Arabic which made me determined henceforward to abandon the classical language and to write in demotic Egyptian. Adonis's poem is merciless about the misplaced pride taken in this language and its terrible political traditions. It makes clear why the educated chatter of intellectuals seemed so vacuous and vapid. The reason why I opted to translate *Othello* into vernacular is thus clear: to enable ordinary people to read great writers in the language they learn at the breast and in which they spend their life from birth to death.

People who are alive owe their life to the pen. Not because authors endow them with 'self-consciousness'. People – it is enough to listen to their jokes – have all the knowledge they need about the passion for tyranny, the despotism of government, the hierarchical distribution of wealth and power among classes and the falsity inherent in all glorification.[4] If truth is more than a matter of chattering, then great pens are its strong refuge, and whoever faces the truth fears no authority.

We are one of the civilisations that invented writing more than five thousand years ago.[5] The state monopolised it and made of it an esoteric art reserved for its scribes. The result was that we remain largely illiterate; perhaps the percentage of our peasants who can read and write does not exceed that of the Athenian citizens in the fifth century BC.

Written in a 'higher' if not sacred language, works about ideas were similarly constituted as a separate domain to which ordinary people had no access. The result was that the state could safely eliminate any writer who dared to contradict the prevailing orthodoxies, and that writers, just like the old scribes, only survived within the established order. One may wonder whether writing in a language reserved for an elite was not the biggest trap – and a narcissistic one at that – into which our writers fell; they became a class of Brahmans who shared no common tongue with the 'vulgar'.[6]

Who could imagine the destiny of Europe if Latin had remained the language of literature, science, philosophy and theology? The end of Latin's linguistic hegemony is worth considering in this context.

The first people in Europe to write in a language whose grammar no one needed to go to school in order to understand were the 'fools',[7] i.e. love poets. They appeared in the south of France, where two languages were spoken, and in Italy, where there were dozens of different dialects. Dante followed suit. His proclaimed master was Virgil whom he considered to be 'the prince of poets'. He realised that the greatest poetry, which meant to him Greek and Latin poetry, was that which was submitted to the rules of the art or, as Bayram[8] put it,

> O art if you had rules and texts
> You would be as the shining stars in the sky.

He therefore decided to write in the vernacular a book about poetry, comparable to Horatius's *Art of Poetry*. The book's title was *De vulgari eloquentia*.[9]

Dante begins with the distinction between a primary common language which we learn without studying, simply by imitating our governesses, and a secondary language which the Romans called 'grammatical'. This distinction once made, he adds: 'Of these two kinds of language, the more noble is the vernacular.'[10] As we can learn from Botterill, this simple sentence contains the 'declaration of independence' of the European languages.[11]

Dante explains his reasons: 'first, because it was the language originally used by the human race; second, because the whole world employs it, though with different pronunciations and using different words; and third, because it is natural to us, while the other is, in contrast, artificial.'[12]

Dante was writing specifically about Italian and Latin but his reflections on the politics of writing have a universal character. He was thus led after his initial declaration in favour of the vernacular to define first language's function and then its history.

The first definition is worth quoting:

> Since, therefore, human beings are moved not by their natural instinct but by reason, and since that reason takes diverse forms in individuals, according to their capacity for discrimination, judgement, or choice – to the point where it appears that almost everyone enjoys the existence of a unique species – I hold that we can never understand the actions or feelings of others by reference to our own, as the baser animals can. Nor is it given to us to enter into each other's minds by means of spiritual reflection, as the angels do, because the human spirit is so weighed down by the heaviness and density of the mortal body.
>
> So it was necessary that the human race, in order for its members to communicate their conceptions among themselves, should have some signal based on reason and perception.[13]

Clearly, what is meant by 'reason' here is intelligible meaning (the signified); by 'perception', the perceptible sound that articulates it (the signifier). As for language's history, Dante was content to retell the story of Nimrod, who prompted humans to build a tower that would reach heaven. Their punishment was that God destroyed their common language and created a Babel of different tongues.

After these theoretical preliminaries, Dante asks (and here his book's political and not merely literary objective becomes plain) what language, amongst at least fourteen languages in Italy, deserves to be the language of government, or rather the language that could unify Italy in the absence of a unified political authority. It is worth noting that his criterion was neither beauty nor practical utility, but the suitability of the language for poetry. In his view, the echoes and strength of poetic language would far outstrip the domain of poetry and even of any aesthetic conception of language to inform the tensions of real life, its battles and ambiguities. With this Dante begins, in the second part of the book, some pages of linguistic analysis and literary critique which constitute the first examples of such study in the European Middle Ages. But the book remains unfinished, it stops in the middle of a sentence; most probably because Dante realised that the problem would not be resolved through theoretical comparisons, it needed a concrete example. He thus dedicated his efforts to the *Divine Comedy* which is still considered the greatest poetic work in the history of European literature and a work that had a determining effect on the Italian language that we now know.

If we look to Eastern Europe, particularly Russia, we shall find that the Russians mainly owe their identity not to the state, nor the land, nor even to religion, but to a dream of Russia which was elaborated by such great writers as Pushkin, Gogol and Dostoevsky.

I assume the reader will say that the comparison between us, Arabs, and the Europeans underestimates the fact that Arabic is not only the language of literature but also that of the Koran.

The answer to this is that if the Koran draws its dignity from being the basis of all Islam, it is also the case that Islam was adopted by many nations that spoke languages other than Arabic, while many Arabic speakers are Christians or Jews.

If this is the case, why should Islam be responsible for political systems that lasted thousands of years before its revelation to Mohammed, systems in which power was never peacefully transmitted: once a ruler came to power, he never left until he died or was murdered?

Moreover, as Euripides' quotation suggests, religion is so rooted in the necessities of social life that it would be dishonest to identify it with any political system. It is rather those political systems that make use of religion as a source of their legitimacy.

My translation of *Othello* into spoken Egyptian was meant to show that spoken Arabic, as well as any living language, has all the ingredients that make it possible to get an admirable literature out of it.[14] I chose Shakespeare because his greatness is indisputable. If it is possible to translate him into our mother tongue, disdainfully disparaged as 'vulgar', then the proof is given that our mother tongue too can attain the 'sublime'.

Why *Othello*? Because Othello speaks as if he were constantly looking in a mirror to check that his image has all the perfections that fascinate the eye and please society. The reason for an existence enthralled by such an ideal image is articulated by Othello when he says, thanks to Shakespeare's divine intuition: 'O curse of marriage!/ That we can call these delicate creatures ours,/ And not their appetites.'[15] Othello thus betrays his inability to understand, or his incapacity to admit, that desire is a gift: he is not content with having obtained Desdemona's desire; what he wants is to possess it so that the beloved may not take it back or turn it to some other object, as if it were a house, a field or a cow. This of course is impossible unless she is transformed into an icon, a statue or an inert corpse; and in fact he does kill her. The difference between him and Iago is that Iago makes no mystery of his destructive drives, while Othello's attachment to the fantasy of his own perfection, which otherwise would have made him a comic character, is so absolute that it allows him to murder.

As a matter of fact, this fascination with the ideal, which goes beyond what we may call the legitimate desire to seduce and becomes the desire to master the Other's desire as such, is very far from unnatural. It has its roots in the fascination exercised at the dawn of life by the figure known as the imaginary or ideal father, a fascination that it may take a whole lifetime to dissipate both in its conscious and its unconscious effects. Without indulging in the subtleties of the distinction between the ideal father and the father ideal, I will simply refer the reader to Freud's description, in his book on group psychology, of the first identifications of the child with his or her father, as well as to my chapter on the ideal father in *Etudes sur l'Oedipe*.[16] There is no doubt that my choice of *Othello* as the text to translate into my mother tongue was as much a result of my experience of psychoanalysis as it was of my belated discovery of Egypt.

Now, we Arabs live in societies where political power, with all its unmistakably farcical character, does not follow the will of the majority but that of the monarch, and the monarch is supposed to incarnate a fatherly ideal. It is true that there is no harm in ideals as long as the person who professes them makes an effort to live up to them. There are also perfectly good ideals such as to do one's work well, to speak rationally, to judge fairly even against oneself, et cetera. However, all these nice distinctions are easily forgotten when political power is submitted to an authority which itself submits to no law or treaty comparable, say, to the treaty that King Edward signed in 1297 and that constituted the basis of the British parliament.[17] More than any other play I know, *Othello* teaches us to temper this natural infatuation for ideals that annihilates thought.

It is worth noting finally that translating *Othello* into spoken Arabic posed no difficulties other than those that occur when translating such a work into any language: the metaphors that lose their beauty and impact because the metaphorical word does not evoke the same associations in the mind of the reader of the translated text; the mental switches based on double meanings; the metonymies that lose their meaning in a different cultural context; the differences in the syntactic structures that call for a different phrasing; the ellipses that have to be made explicit; the idiomatic expressions that have to be reworked in order to touch the reader's linguistic sensibility, and so on. There is of course something that no translation can reproduce – 'Othello's music', as one critic called it – because this music emanates from the sounds of the English language itself, but I tried as much as possible to produce a translation that could be heard as well as read.[18] If aiming at perfection could be considered as an incentive to do better, I can say that I do hope to see someone better my translation. The important point for any translator is that there are no two words belonging to two different languages that have exactly the same meaning. As Richards remarked, the use of any word, from an article to a proper name, especially its poetic use, sets in motion the whole system of the language with its semantic implications, which give the word its unique resonance, its specific weight.[19]

It may be even more important to notice, as Yves Bonnefois said in his last book on Shakespeare and Yeats, that every language has a certain philosophy inscribed in it, which speech presupposes without making explicit. For example, French looks at universals first, then at particulars because they are considered as examples and proofs of the universal. This is why dramatic conflict, for example in Racine's plays, has to be a rational conflict like the one between love and duty or between the betrayal of a tyrant and that of a friend. Things go the opposite way in English, where the individual takes the lead: through the incomprehensible conflict of which an individual is the victim, as in Hamlet's hesitation, we may have some understanding of the universal laws. It follows that translating Shakespeare into French does not mean making him look French; on the contrary, such a translation is a struggle to make the French language comply with a different philosophy. The same applies to translation into Arabic. I have never heard anyone talk of the implicit philosophy of Arabic, but if I were asked, I would say that to speak Arabic is to enter a well-ordered universe where every being has its proper place and both individual being and general universe are protected.[20] This is a philosophy that reality may refute thousands of times without ever changing it since it constitutes the latent premises of communication. Translation into Arabic should not follow the so-called ideal of 'Arabisation'; on the contrary, translating consists in using the language in order to free ourselves from the limits imposed on us by that language.

Notes

A first draft of this chapter was published as an introduction to my translation into spoken Arabic of Shakespeare's *Othello* (Egypt: Angelo Edition, 1998).

1 Euripides, *Bacchae*, ll. 168–71, trans. David Franklin (Cambridge: Cambridge University Press, 2000). *Bacchae* is generally considered to be the first work ever written in sociology and the foundation stone of that science.
2 *The Muqaddimah: An Introduction to History*, trans. Franz Rosenthal (London: Routledge and Kegan Paul, 1967).
3 Leo Strauss, *Persecution and the Art of Writing* (Glencoe, IL: Free Press, 1952).
4 I may add that they are just as well aware of the subversive character of writing. During a conversation with a taxi driver in Cairo, I was led to tell him a joke that was popular in Nasser's time – before he was born. It is the story of a young man caught sticking posters on a wall. He is led to the police station; after the usual beating up, he is confronted with the posters. But to the police's surprise, these turn out to be blank sheets ... At this point in the story the taxi driver roared with laughter: 'They asked him where he hid the writing!' This is a wittier punchline than in the original story, which ended with the police asking what he wanted to say and the young man signifying that there was much to say and nothing to be said.
5 I am referring to syllabic and alphabetic writing. In fact, there is no human society that does not have some form of writing. Writing did not wait for the analysis of language to appear; it prepared the way for that analysis. Cf. M. Safouan, *L'Inconscient et son scribe* (Paris: Seuil, 1982), ch. 1.

6   Unless translated into foreign languages, no Arab writer earns his living by the sale of his books. The great majority work in newspapers, publishing houses and other institutions that belong to the state.

7   I am alluding to the great pre-Islamic poet Madjnoun Laïla, the fool of Laïla, who devoted his poetical genius to the woman he loved, according to a tradition of 'virginal love', which some authors consider as one of the sources of medieval courtly love. He inspired Aragon's *Le Fou d'Elsa, Poème* (1964).

8   Bayram al-Tunsi (1863–1941) was the first poet in modern Egypt who wrote in spoken Arabic. He thus inaugurated a vigorous movement that remains alive although ignored by the educational system.

9   Dante Alighieri, *De vulgari eloquentia*, ed. and trans. Stephen Botterill (Cambridge: Cambridge University Press, 1996).

10   Ibid., 3.

11   Ibid., xviii.

12   Ibid., 3.

13   Ibid., 7.

14   By 'ingredients' I refer to the two axes of language distinguished by de Saussure: the syntagmatic and paradigmatic. Jakobson baptised them as the axes of substitution and combination and showed how metaphors pertain to the first axis and metonymies to the second.

15   Act III, scene 3, ll. 268–70. There was a debate about this translation that took place in Cairo. Some speakers expressed their astonishment that such a great poet as Shakespeare would tackle such directly sexual matter. One of them, who had not found these lines in the classical Arabic translation he had, looked up the English text – and lo, there they were!

16   Paris: Editions du Seuil, 1974.

17   The first reaffirmation of the Magna Carta, by King Edward. Indeed Europe's history can be summarised in a series of pacts and treaties that led to the division of power between the state and the Church, between the popes, the emperors and the kings, between the kings and the parliaments, or between the legislative, executive and judicial powers. The secret of Europe's strength is the division of power between the different currents of the political society, instead of a monopoly of power being based on a terrifying and hypocritical confusion between political society as such and the community (*Djama'a*), which denotes in the first place the community of the faithful meeting in the mosque (*Djami'*). As a result of this confusion, differences of opinion are treated as differences of creed; those who profess them are considered as 'outsiders' (*Khawaredj*) that *should* be eliminated.

18   The play was actually performed in an Egyptian town, Almansoura. The actors (much more than the actresses) were so thoroughly trained to perform in classical Arabic that they did not feel particularly at ease in their mother tongue. The effect would probably have been different if they played a comedy: comedies are usually acted in the vernacular.

19   Ivor A. Richards, *The Philosophy of Rhetoric* (New York: Oxford University Press, 1936).

20   In his book on pre-Islamic poetry, *Le Voyageur sans Orient: poesie et philosophe des Arabes de l'ère préislamique* (Paris: Sindbad, 1998), Salam Al-Kindy shows that the ontological feeling that inspired this poetry was, rather, that of the ephemeral. If what I say above is true, it means that the Arabic language's philosophy completely changed once Arabic became the language of the state and administration.

5

The Role of Language in the Creation of Culture

A much cited aphorism of the German philosopher Heidegger asserts, 'Language is the house of being. In its home man dwells.' A humorist commented that if that was the case then the housing problem was solved. However, if we put humour aside, it is true that man not only lives in language, but that he is nurtured by it.

The word 'creation' that appears in this chapter's title has two meanings: a thing created and the act of creation. Firstly, nothing in any culture exists that does not owe its existence to language or that is not is perceived thanks to language's mediation. Among things that owe their existence to language, we find beliefs, customs, legends, poems, oaths, pacts, titles, constitutions, prohibitions, laws, et cetera. As for things that are only perceived through the mediation of language, I would say that the theory according to which things once existed 'in themselves', waiting for the first man to give them their names only exists in some cosmic epics or religious legends; that is, once again, in language. The fact is that no man ever existed except in a 'universe' where things were already named and classified in kinds and species, whether tangibles (such as metals, plants or animals) or non tangibles (such as the four directions, or virtues and vices). These classifications vary from culture to culture, that is from language to language, even in areas where sensation would seem to dictate the classification – as with, for example, colours. In brief, it is thanks to language that thought pervades reality and is impregnated with it.

Moreover, each individual receives at birth a name, usually chosen before he or she is put in the cradle. This naming entails a number of duties that precede all choice: family and religious duties as well as duties towards one's own class, tribe or nation. These duties give individuals their identity, define their presence to themselves and to others, make a responsible subject out of them and direct their destiny.

Nonetheless, despite the weight of these first identifications, the birth of an individual means – at least in principle and unless they identify themselves with these very first identifications to the point of being imprisoned in and by them – the birth of a new gaze, a new possibility of considering the received culture and eventually of developing it. Here we need to talk of cultural creativity as an act of transmission that can only take place thanks to language. In chapter 3 we distinguished between a stagnant transmission such as unchanging methods of agriculture and irrigation in Egypt down the centuries, and a creative transmission that occurs for the first time with the appearance of the class of 'intellectuals' in twelfth-century Europe. Everything depends on education policy and methods.

This was why my decision to translate *Othello* into vernacular spoken Egyptian had nothing to do with personal preference. The fact is that I, like everyone else, grew up with a love, nay a veneration, of classical Arabic. To read or write it was to enter a solemn world, full of glory, the glory of the past with all its history, a history full of the pride of affiliation. Nevertheless, whatever one's education and affiliation, they are no reason to favour one language over another, whether we consider that language from the point of view of the people who speak it or from the point of view of its inner structure.

First, imagine an idea with no word to express it in a certain language. This idea can belong to any domain: it can be religious, such as sacrifice and sin; economic, such as salary and price; scientific, such as inertia and gravity; or philosophic, such as existence and essence . . . It is clear that for the users of this language, such a nameless idea will not constitute the content of any commandment or prohibition, it will not represent the goal of any action, nor will it be the object of meditation or reflection. In other words, everyhing will go on in the society without anybody feeling the lack or the need of this nameless idea. This is why, as Saussure noted, every society is content with its own language and why all attempts to create one 'rational' international language as, for example, with Esperanto, have failed. Language is the only thing with which man can be fully satisfied.

Second, with regard to language's inner structure, we know since Saussure that each language is constructed according to two dimensions which he called the syntagmatic and paradigmatic dimensions. The first, which we may call horizontal, is the dimension in which words are combined with each other so that they may form a discourse. This is also the dimension in which a word brings to mind another word thanks to the connections between their given or received significations. This is the dimension which Jakobson called the axis of combination and this is the axis of metonymy. The example we all learned when we were young is that 'a lot of ashes' is a metonym for generosity, since a generous person, in desert life, always had a big fire in his house and fire makes ashes. This example shows clearly how a metonym in one culture may lose its meaning in another culture. If we look at books of rhetoric in the West, the first example of metonymy is 'thirty sails' for 'thirty ships'. This example makes very clear that the connection is a connection between the two words in the first place since, in fact, each ship, as Lacan remarked, has more than one sail.

As to the second dimension, which Jakobson called the axis of substitution or selection, it represents the way in which words are, one might say, vertically arranged. This is the dimension where we select a word that will suit the intentional meaning although language always offers the possibility of an inspiration in excess of an intention. Indeed this is, as Jakobson noted, the axis of metaphor. The classic example ever since Aristotle is 'the evening of life' for 'old age'. Far from saying the same thing in other words, 'the evening of life' teases out ambiguous meanings for 'old age', depending on whether you think of darkness or of the peace of dusk.

These two dimensions characterise language as such. Any language thus has a place for poetical imagination and wit, for intimation as well as for standard speech. There are no vulgar and no noble languages; eloquence and vulgarity are possible in every language.

It is true that, having distinguished between the 'grammatical language' learned in school, and the vulgar language learned at the breast, Dante stated that the second was the better. But given his familiarity with Aristotle,[1] Dante would almost certainly agree that every language is learned by 'natural disposition' and, given the articulated character of the human voice, that it is transposable into alphabetical letters (*éngrámmatos*); writing is not a technique added to language from outside, but one of its intrinsic dimensions. Dante's argument was not about languages but about a politics of writing, and a vicious politics at that, for it was designed to perpetuate the political rule of the Church.

Indeed, the reason why I chose to translate *Othello* into vulgar Egyptian was linked to this question: why did Arab culture vanish to the point that it barely participates in the world's contemporary life (except to a slight extent in literature), whereas Western culture flourished to the point of penetrating into all the world's cultures and forcing every culture to adapt to the West if it wished to survive? The conclusion I was led to has the advantage, I dare say, of having been proved by history.

Near the middle of the nineteenth century, Alexis de Tocqueville wrote a book that was translated into many languages. It is a painful proof of our backwardness that it is still not translated into Arabic. In this book, *Democracy in America*, de Tocqueville came to the conclusion that the world's future would be determined by the struggle between two giants, Russia and America. He was in little doubt that America would win thanks to its powerful *political regime*.

Before considering that regime, let us reflect briefly on communism. Communism was the political project to accomplish the historically promised victory of the proletariat as a prelude to the advent of global equality and justice. But it became clear that the truth of this one-class society was a one-party regime having as its head a 'secretary general' who was the one to decide right from wrong even in such matters as linguistics and biology, let alone the works of Marx and Engels. If one may describe as a theocracy any regime that refers to a text which is to be interpreted by a single authority, and which thus guarantees that all you need to do is open the text and the Truth will be there waiting for you, then the Soviet Union may be described as having been a 'secular theocracy' whose Bible was Marx and Engels's *Manifesto* as interpreted by Joseph Stalin.

The defeat of such a regime was predictable since putting an end to all differences and transforming society into a community of the faithful is the product of an idealism that is better described as madness, in the sense that it has lost all connection with reality. It is impossible to eliminate all differences between men because there are no universal principles or criteria which can be used to solve all problems. This applies even to abstract sciences. There is more than one logic according to whether you accept the principle of excluded middle or reject it. There is more than one geometry according to whether you admit or refuse to admit the postulate that parallel lines do not meet. So what about such social and political problems as: do we declare war on another state in the name of human rights or do we respect the agreements stipulated in treaties? Do we submit to a stronger and richer nation to guarantee our relative welfare or do we solely abide by the principle of independence and refuse submission whatever the price? These different options cannot be considered independently of the different interests within a society. The fact is there is no human society that does not harbour the seeds of discord, which is to say the possibility of civil war. The price for achieving a homogeneity where there is no place for otherness had to be concentration camps. It is true that the Soviet regime gave shelter to each citizen, but all those outside the party felt that their lives depended on the salary the state gave them and not on their own activity, since their safety depended on their silence. That is why there was no solidarity between the great majority of the citizens and the state, between the governed and the government, as became clear when the regime collapsed. The iron curtain which was supposed to protect the people from the lies of capitalist propaganda was of no use after the invention of the transistors which enabled anyone to buy a small pocket radio and to listen to news from any part of the world. I happened to meet an Egyptian peasant who had a small radio hanging on his plough and was listening to the news. When I asked him about what he was listening to, he answered:

'To the Voice of America.'
'And why do you listen to the Voice of America?'
'Because they tell the truth.'
'And how do you know they tell the truth?'
'Because they say the contrary of what is said here, and here they are liars!'

I imagine this was the same with Russian peasants or those among them who survived the draconian collectivisation.

As a matter of fact, one may say that, far from being an utterly new phenomenon in world history, the Soviet state merely reran the example of those archaic states like that of the Nile valley. To leave that valley meant losing any possibility of life. To live in the valley meant access to plentiful water. Therefore, according to the commonly accepted theory, to avoid generalised fighting over this vital element, it was necessary to rely on a third party, that is on a ruler or a government which monopolised the right to distribute the water, as well as the right to use violence if necessary, in order to enforce its rules. Hobbes's theory seems to apply here: man is a wolf to man and this means that men cannot live together unless every individual renounces his particular will and submits it to a third party. But the fact is that the idea of an irrevocable contract according to which the subjects transfer all authority to one sovereign, an idea which indeed makes of the people the ultimate source of legitimacy, had no part in the genesis of the archaic states. The first characteristic of the archaic state, a characteristic easy to detect in our present-day 'republics' with their immovable presidents, is that the sovereign draws his authority and legitimacy not from the constitution and the people but in the last resort from religion inasmuch as it organises what I may call the 'natural' belief in the order of the sacred.

The second characteristic is the indivisibility of power. The sovereign accepts no rival. Any opposition is considered as a diminishing not only of his power but of his very being.

The third characteristic is the absence of all real control of the sovereign's authority and, consequently, of any rule of law or civil society.

The fourth characteristic is that the sovereign's first job, before even defence, the economy or national independence, is to guarantee 'stability', that is the permanence of his rule. Nowadays, once a president comes to power after a coup d'état, as was the case with Nasser, or after the death or assassination of his predecessor, as was the case with Sadat and Mubarak, he customarily renews his rule in a display of modernity with elections that award him a victory with 99 per cent of the vote. But the fact is that these modern archaic states enjoy a kind of existence comparable to that of Monsieur Valdemar who, according to Edgar Allan Poe's tale, happened to die while he was under hypnosis but who kept an appearance of life as long as the hypnosis lasted. At the first blow, they collapse.

America's force is due to its institutions. The 'Founding Fathers', men such as James Madison, John Adams, Thomas Jefferson and James Wilson, read the best and most advanced writings available to eighteenth-century European political analysis, such as John Locke's *Essay Concerning Human Understanding* and his two essays on government; Adam Smith's *Wealth of Nations* and *Theory of Moral Sentiments*, as well as Montesquieu's *Défense de l'esprit des lois*. They not only carefully read them but were, at the same time, shrewd politicians. Their ambition, as Tocqueville explained, was not to transform human nature, but rather to enable men to transform nature for man's benefit. They knew that human nature was ambitious, spiteful and greedy, but they also believed that men were good enough to be able to rule themselves. The most difficult trick in establishing a 'government which is to be exercised by men over men' was, according to Madison, to find mechanisms to control those who govern, just as there are mechanisms to control the governed. This was the inspiration for the Declaration of Independence on 4 July 1776 and for the Constitution which they wanted the nation to love always and which receives that veneration without which even the wisest and most freedom-loving government would probably not possess the required stability. This commitment to a republican regime limited and controlled by the law and to a written and trustworthy constitution, and above all the belief in the sacred character of individual freedom enabled the Founding Fathers to create the longest-lasting constitution in the world. In addition, if we look to a European nation such as the British, we shall find that, because of a long history of fighting the government, the people's attitude towards it is not wholly free from a mixture of caution and suspicion, whereas the Americans, having no such a history, trust their government completely. This strong bond between the nation and the state was entirely lacking under the Soviet regime.

The influence of eighteenth-century authors on the Founding Fathers is another proof of the importance of writers in the formation, if not the creation, of nations; an importance they would never have had if they did not write in a language open to all those who spoke it – which does not mean that they were read by all of them. From this point of view, we may say that Montesquieu, who was the most penetrating analyst of political institutions, was the heir of du Bellay, the poet who, with his *Défense et illustration de la langue française*, may be said to have introduced the principle of linguistic humanism in France as Dante did in Italy.

It is a widespread belief that this principle should not be applied to the Arabic of the Koran which is the language of God. But this is a patently false belief if not an impious one, since it applies to God the limitations that afflict human beings. It is clear that in choosing His prophet, God chooses the language in which He wants to convey His message. He talked Hebrew to Abraham and Moses and He talked Arabic with His last prophet. The choice of language is secondary. As to the reasons for the choice of His prophets, we may suppose, although we do not know if God's actions are motivated the way our actions are, that He chose the men who were most faithful to Him and most unshakable in their faith. In fact, if we consider the way God took into account the limitations of human nature and the fact that the Arabic idioms spoken in Cairo and Rabat are as different from the language of the Qureish[2] and from each other as French and Italian are from Latin, we should translate the Koran into these tongues.

Another argument which Arab intellectuals love to repeat is that spoken Arabic is inappropriate for any work that aspires to thought or culture. But this argument merely reflects the infatuation with classical Arabic. The fact is that the difficulties I met in translating Shakespeare's *Othello* into spoken Arabic were no more nor less great than those I met in translating Freud or Hegel into classical Arabic.[3] I have already referred to the process of translating *Othello*. All I wish to add here is that the difficulties occurred not only at the level of vocabulary and style but also at the level of syntax. There is no doubt that the syntax of spoken Arabic is simpler than classical Arabic, but this simplicity is by no means a deficiency. Indeed, for any serious translation, spoken Arabic may be more suitable than classical Arabic.

A third and final argument which is almost universally accepted is that classical Arabic unites us as Arabs. But those who support this argument must admit that there is more agreement among European countries than the Arab states have ever been able to achieve. Despots never agree. If we translated into our mother tongues, that might help us to achieve both greater self-understanding and greater understanding of others.[4]

There are two opposing conceptions of translation. According to the first, the aim of translation is to subdue the text to one's culture or, as the current metaphor goes, to 'digest' it. According to the second, the aim is, on the contrary, to accustom and subdue one's 'mentality' to the foreign thought that exists in the text to be translated. A translation made according to the first – which we call Arabisation if into Arabic, Gallicising if into French, and so forth – is deaf and it would be better not to undertake it at all, since it serves only to reinforce our prejudices while giving us no access to what may be new in a different thought. Each language presupposes some concepts that pervade all communication. The more glory and veneration time bestows on a language, the tighter the control of these preconceptions is on the brain and the more difficult it is to revise them. Because of its freshness, spoken language may make it easier to have access to other cultural categories and to strike neologisms, a procedure that sometimes proves to be necessary. A good example of this is the English of Shakespeare which is constantly creating new words for new thoughts in a tongue which had yet to be codified.

Let me give some examples where the prestige of classical Arabic has led to very inadequate translation in the field of political theory.

(1) The Latin word *res publica* was translated as 'common interest' (*almaslaha al'amma*). It thus lost its meaning, which was reduced to the rather moral and trivial distinction between common and private or egoistical interests. It would be better to translate it by the common or public 'cause' (*alqadiya al'amma*). Imagine a society that faced the following question: do we build a canal to link the sea to a particular

river or not? Some would agree because it would revive the area; some will disagree because they fear the competitive effects of this revival. The common character of the cause does not imply the negation of the private interests. On the contrary, it presupposes them. A politician may be defined as a man who makes public or common causes his occupation, not in order to defend the common interests, but on behalf of the class or group he represents, if not his personal interests.

(2) The word 'sovereignty' was translated in Arabic as *siyada*, which means 'domination' (literally: 'mastership' or *Herrlichkeit*), whereas its true meaning, at least according to Karl Schmitt's definition, is the 'right to take decisions in the last resort'. The translation leaves us only with the primitive, dual relation of master and slave, whereas what is at stake is a political conception of decision.

(3) Aristotle's book on *Politics* was translated as *siyasa*, a word derived from the root *sasa* which means, literally, 'to deal with' or 'to lead'. It completely obliterates the meaning of Aristotle's enterprise, which was not concerned with leadership but with 'the things of the city (*polis*)', the city being a state. The book searches for a definition of the constitution and of the citizen (a word for which we have no translation, the current translation (*mouwaten*) meaning, rather, 'compatriot'). It also examines the question of the best government (probably owing to his theory of the 'mean' he thought it would be government by the middle class) and other similar matters. The translation we have is a pure 'Arabisation'.

Translation into spoken Arabic not only contributes to enlightenment of the common people, but it also contributes to the liberation of our thinking processes. No culture can develop without communicating with other cultures, and communication means translation. We may count in tens the number of books translated into Arabic each year, while translations into Polish or Japanese are counted in their thousands. Even if we have been colonised by the West, a fact that does not encourage us to have towards Western countries the minimum of friendship required in all cultural exchange, our poor production in the field of translation is a sign that something in addition to the balance of power is at work. Indeed, the poverty of translation is a sure indication that there is something deeply rotten in our whole contemporary culture, based as it is on a politics of writing which has lasted for thousands of years. It is this politics that we have to overthrow if we wish to have a share in our destiny, that is if we want to have a creative, historical existence.

Notes

A first draft of this chapter was delivered in 1998 as a lecture to the Faculty of Letters, University of Mansoura, where I had been invited by the Department of Psychology.

1   Cf. Lorenzo Minio-Paluello, 'Dante's Reading of Aristotle', in *The World of Dante: Essays on Dante and his Times*, ed. Cecil Grayson (Oxford: Clarendon Press, 1980), 61–80.
2   The name of the tribe into which Mohammed was born.
3   I translated the section on consciousness from Hegel's *The Phenomenology of Spirit*. My difficulties in finding a publisher, the absence of any reaction from the Arab intelligentsia and the dismal sales dissuaded me from completing the project. The translation of Freud's *The Interpretation of Dreams*, although it received no reviews, was on the contrary a big success. As far as I know, it is still on sale, almost half a century after its first publication in January 1959.
4   Probably owing to their geographical isolation, with the western and eastern deserts on each side of the Nile valley, Egyptians were too conscious of, not to say infatuated with, themselves as Egyptians to identify with a wider circle. Pan-Arabism was first launched by Nasser. His call had a wide and vibrant response not only for historical and religious reasons but also because most of the Arab nations, particularly in the Middle East, were engaged in the struggle against foreign occupation. This book may be considered as an attempt to replace the idea of unity by that of agreement reached on realistic bases and compatible with the recognition of difference.

6

Writing and Power

In his *Tristes tropiques*[1] Claude Lévi-Strauss dedicated a few pages to the topic of writing and its role in human societies. These pages aroused enormous interest and are still a topic for discussion. 'Writing', he wrote,

> is a strange invention ... The only phenomenon with which writing has always been concomitant is the creation of cities and empires, that is, the integration of large numbers of individuals into a political system, and their grading into castes and classes. Such, at any rate, is the typical pattern of development to be observed from Egypt to China, at the time when writing first emerged: it seems to have favoured the exploitation of human beings rather than their enlightenment ... The use of writing for disinterested purposes, and as a source of intellectual and aesthetic pleasure, is a secondary result, and more often than not it may even be turned into a means of strengthening, justifying or concealing the other.[2]

The least one can say about this opinion is that it applies to a good number of human societies but not to all of them. The role writing had in the archaic states such as Egypt, at the dawn of history on the banks of the great rivers, is different from the one it had in Greek cities, such as Athens. Before considering the case of Egypt, let us examine the case of Athens.

Writing appeared in the Greek world before 750 BC. The Greeks took the Phoenician alphabet and added five more letters for the vowels. In the last years of the seventh century (around 621 BC), Draco promulgated his law on homicide. The importance of this law is that it established the city as the only authority which could impose punishments and put an end to the *lex talionis* that was customary among aristocratic families. Plutarch claims that Draco's laws stipulated death penalties for so many crimes other than murder that they were said to be written in blood and not in ink. Draco himself, when asked about the reason for this severity, replied that in his view small crimes deserved the death penalty and that he was unable to find a more severe penalty for greater crimes. Afterwards, Solon (594 BC) promulgated many laws, the most important of which was the law of tax relief, which aimed at abolishing the right of landowners to enslave indebted farmers to work on their land. What is important from our perspective is that Draco's and Solon's laws were written and engraved on pieces of wood that revolved around an axis so that they could be read on all four sides. During the sixth century, laws engraved on stones increased, as well as treaties and texts defining the units of measurement and the values of scales and money; also census lists, names of those killed in battle, offerings presented to temples and gods, et cetera. This did not signal the appearance of a bureaucracy, because the written texts, even if preserved, were not stored in one place; most of the time, they were destroyed when the purpose of their having been written down was exhausted, as when a loan had been repaid, for example. In general, the idea of the state as an independent entity separate from and in control of individuals was foreign to Greek cities because the citizens considered themselves to be the city: it was they, at least theoretically, who proposed the laws and took the decisions, and it was they, during periods of democratic rule, who acted as judges. It was of course impossible for all citizens to leave their work and assemble in order to judge each case. The search for a solution to this problem led to the idea of 'representation' for the first time in history: they decided to choose a number of citizens to represent all the others and to judge cases for a limited time. Hence the use of writing in the city did not take the form of well preserved documents essential to bureaucracy, but that of public announcements on stones put in the open air for everyone to see. The citizen who wanted to know the value of a piece of money went to the counting house, the one who wanted to know the date of a feast went to the temple, even treaties were 'published' in specific places.

This does not mean that all citizens knew how to write. The feeling prevailed, rather, that writing had an intrinsic dignity because it defied time, and written texts had a sacred aura; we need only think of Moses' tablets. In general, we may say that Athenians in the classical era perceived the law, unlike us, as something visible that had a physical existence. The important point, however, is that writing in the sixth century was not monopolised by the aristocrats and the scribes who were in the service of the state. Potters, sculptors, bronze specialists and other craftsmen had some idea of it, and any ambitious or rich citizen could learn it, as there was a general consensus that every citizen had the right to know it because every citizen had the right to know the law. It is true, according to Aristotle's pertinent remark, that the poor do not usually think of obtaining important positions; the financial, diplomatic and military jobs were always in the hands of the rich aristocrats who had enough time to spend on public affairs. However, it was the mass of all citizens, rich and poor, who chose the officials, defined their responsibilities and judged their actions.

This raises the following question: was the relative expansion of writing among craftsmen and professionals due to the development of the city or the other way round? We are most probably looking at two related phenomena, each one cause and consequence of the other. What is certain is that after the end of the archaic period in the sixth century BC and the beginning of the classical era in the fifth century BC, the use of writing increased considerably. It is also certain that the appearance of democracy gave each citizen a greater sense of his own value, which made him want to learn to write. A strong indication is the decision in 480 BC not to exile any citizen unless 6,000 citizens writing their names on a piece of clay or slate agreed. This is good evidence that primary schools to teach reading and writing probably existed. It is worth noting that exile (*ostraica*) was a measure adopted in case a leader became so popular that he might be tempted to take all the power into his own hands.The exile could not exceed ten years and the exiled citizen retained the right to his property. In other words, exile was a procedure intended to protect democracy, analogous to the fixed term limits on presidents in the United States. It is said that a man from the countryside came to vote to exile Aristides. He did not know how to write Aristides' name and asked his neighbour to do it for him. The neighbour happened to be Aristides himself. 'Has Aristides', he asked, 'done anything to you?' The man answered: 'I have never even seen him, but I am fed up to the back teeth with perpetually hearing him described as "the honest"; you never hear anyone simply say "Aristides", his name is always followed by "the honest".' The importance of this story is not whether it is true or not, but in its implications. It shows that the Greeks were already aware of the danger of a leader so virtuous and so exceptional that he was elected and re-elected over and over again because it was considered impossible 'to find someone to replace him'. As if the country was fertile before his birth and became sterile after it.

The use of writing expanded between 479 and 323 BC, especially in trade and legal proceedings. In 340 BC, a law to forbid the filing of any case without referring to a written contract was issued in Athens. This applied to civil procedures as well: freeing a slave necessitated a written document, to ensure that the decision could not be revoked. In the last quarter of the fifth century BC, legal arguments had to be written down. In the beginning, the scribes who assisted the legal proceedings wrote them, but after 370 BC each party was responsible for writing his own. Under Demosthenes, a law specified that, in certain cases, testimony had to be presented in a written form, although that testimony had to be read orally in the presence of witnesses to verify truthfulness. We can imagine the increase in the use of writing as Athens expanded its empire, and the consequent need for correspondence between the centre and the periphery, as well as the greater complexity of administrative procedures, especially regarding the efficiency of tax collection and the establishment of creditor and debtor lists, and so forth.

While this expansion was going on, writing began to be used for purposes other than those Aristotle described as 'useful'. The writing of history started. We have all heard of Herodotus, the 'father of history'; it is certain, however, that Herodotus himself relied on writings that preceded him. He finished his book in 420 BC and Thucydides came thirty years later. Greater respect for documents began with Thucydides, although this did not mean that he considered manuscripts to be the only source of history. There is no doubt that the writing of history increased the importance of reading and engendered the desire to study a past beyond the limits of memory. In addition, there were Aeschylus's tragedies and the deep impact they made on Athenians, especially in the case of *The Persians*, in which Athenians heard for the first time a dazzling description of the Greeks' defeat of the Persians in the naval battle at Salamis. Aeschylus also wrote *The Suppliant Women*, in which its Athenian audience could enjoy a comparison of democracy and despotism, with a clear preference shown for the freedom of a people living in a democracy. This explosion of writing has as a consequence the appearance of a new trade: the book trade (420–410 BC). Private and public libraries grew up alongside the blossoming of the theatre and the love the Athenians had for it, which caused Plato to describe democracy – and he was one of its enemies – as a 'theatrocracy'. The book also developed as part of the growth in scientific and mathematical thought, both elements of the tremendous development of philosophy which claimed the power to criticise every aspect of life, from the testimony of the senses to democracy itself. It is therefore no wonder that the development of reading as an intellectual activity pursued for its own sake, led to writing itself becoming the subject of much thought, dividing authors into supporters and opponents.

One of the most enthusiastic supporters was Diodorus, as is shown in the following lines:

> it is by means of this that the most important and the most useful of life's business is completed – votes, letters, testaments, laws, and everything else which puts life on the right track. For who could write a worthy encomium of literacy? For it is by means of writing alone that the dead are brought to the minds of the living, and it is through the written word that people who are spatially very far apart communicate with each other as if they were nearby. As to treaties made in time of war between peoples or kings, the safety provided by the written word is the best guarantee of the survival of the agreement. Generally it is this alone which preserves the finest sayings of wise men and the oracles of the gods, as well as philosophy and all of culture, and hands them on to succeeding generations for all time. Therefore, while it is true that nature is the cause of life, the cause of the *good* life is education based on the written word.[3]

As for the opponents, it is not surprising that Herodotus and Thucydides are first amongst them since they learned from their own work how unreliable writing could be. And Aristophanes, in *The Birds*, describes writing attributed to the gods as lies and defamations. However, it is Plato's thoughts about writing which make clear the link between writing and politics. In *Phaedrus*, Plato made his well known threefold attack on writing.[4]

First, Plato attacks the notion that writing develops memory. Quite the contrary, according to him, it weakens memory by leading people to rely on external signs to validate memory. Thus writing develops recall rather than memory. There are many examples to back up Plato's insight. One example comes from Hawaii where, before the Hawaiians started to read and write, many had memorised the Bible by heart just from listening to it being read aloud.

Second, it is claimed that writing cultivates and refines the mind, but for Plato this is an illusion. Writing is without beginning or end. Anyone who reads in this infinite material may seem to have an opinion on everything while, in fact, lacking good judgement – and this before we even consider the tedious ponderousness of the pedant with great pretensions but no real knowledge.

Third, the last and really scary thing about writing is its resemblance to painting. Writing is like a painting: you cannot expect from it an answer to your question, and it cannot defend itself. When speech is written, it runs on the page without taking into consideration those who understand and those who do not, those to whom it should be addressed and those to whom it should not. Written speech is merely a false imitation of oral speech which, because it is accompanied by knowledge, is written in the mind of the subject.

In spite of this criticism, Plato was the first to plead, in Book 7 of *The Laws*, for the need to establish schools for a mandatory education in his ideal city, where reading and writing should be taught to boys and girls, without any discrimination. The question then arises: how can he so severely criticise writing and, at the same time, promote its teaching?

When writing first appears, it immediately takes the form of revealed truth. There are many proofs of that. The creation of writing, just like the creation of the world itself, was always attributed to one of the gods. This is why archaic states were keen to promote the writing engraved on stones and obelisks, although they knew, or precisely because they knew, that their people were unable to read and they desired to keep them in that position of ignorance. The very fact that it was writing gave it enough prestige to ensure people's submission. But Plato wrote in a society where every citizen was allowed to write, at least theoretically. It is true that the percentage of those who could read did not exceed at most 5 per cent of the farmers and 10 per cent to 20 per cent at most of the free citizens, but the important thing, which I have already noted, is that writing was not a monopoly in the hands of a certain category of the population'; any rich or ambitious man could teach his children how to write, even before the establishment of schools. In brief, Athens was a society where writing surpassed the four useful purposes enumerated by Aristotle: getting money, household administration, education, and political and religious occupations. Writing in Athens became a tool for philosophy, literature (especially poetry and theatre) and history. It thus became possible to think of law (*nomos*) as something relative, depending on the people's will in their societies and not as something revealed; it was similarly possible to consider writing itself and see its liability to lies and errors. The significance of Plato's criticism is thus clear: *to remove from writing its sacred character*. The way to truth is not writing but dialectics, that is the spoken word with its implication of two, or rather three, parties: the speaker, the listener and the language they share. With his criticism, Plato, for the first time in man's history, distilled the notion of rationality as such, free of all mixture with belief. I would say this discovery was as important as that of writing itself. There is no doubt that Plato was aware of the significance of his criticism. As proof I may cite the way he began his criticism by mentioning the Egyptian legend that explained the apparition of writing as a gift from the god Thoth and by imagining a discussion between Thoth and the king of Thebes. Such proof gains its full impact if we remember Plato's constant distinction between the subjects where reason and dialectics have their say and those requiring an appeal to legends and beliefs in order that we may fill up the holes of our ignorance. If he still asked for mandatory teaching of writing, it was because it was necessary for political governance (a duty for free citizens) and for household administration (a duty for women).

It is important to recognise that this first separation between rationality and faith in the field of human thought could never have taken place without the Athenian experience of democracy in the fifth and sixth centuries BC. In order to make this point clear, it is necessary to say a word about what we may call the philosophical postulates of political systems.

There are two methods of thought open to political philosophy. The first starts with the question: what is the ideal system? This question concerns what should be and leaves aside the differences that exist between human societies and within the same society. Of course, erasing all differences and achieving complete homogeneity are only possible in a satirical play, such as Aristophanes' *The Parliament of Women*. The idea of the play is that women disguise themselves as men and, therefore, are able to infiltrate councils and to constitute the majority. Thus, they lavishly issue laws that ban all forms of discrimination and achieve complete equality of rights and obligations, between men and women, the rich and the poor, the young and the old, the ugly and the handsome, slaves and the free, the ignorant and the knowledgeable, and so on. The consequence is that social life becomes impossible – complete homogeneity means continuous strife, with no judge to resolve a dispute. The aim of the ideal city is, therefore, to achieve unity not by erasing differences, but by submitting the lower to the higher. Plato, in his *Republic*, had to produce a model in which function determines submission in a chain of authority right up to the head.

The second road open to political philosophy begins with the question formulated by Aristotle: what is the city? In other words: what is the thing we call city or state?[5] Aristotle observes, if the city were an organic unity, such as a cow, a horse or a person, or if it were even a manmade product, such as a palace or a temple, its unity would be clear and we would not have to seek it. Yet, we talk about the city as if it were a unity, while in fact it is not. It is true that the city unites the different elements constituting it, but it never eliminates the differences. Nor can its unity be compared to that of the human body with the submission of its different members to the head, because nature, says Aristotle, does not give us a man so exceptional that the people can consider him as a god. Moreover, politics, like any practical science, asks questions that do not have one answer; assigning government to philosophers or to men who have 'science', as Plato suggests, would not do. Aristotle, therefore, deems it much better for the city to proceed with a regular change of leaders, because such a change allows the application of different opinions and the correction of errors. This thesis puts an end to another comparison, that is the comparison of the city to a family, since the roles in the latter group are permanent: the government for the father and the submission for the wife and children. The unity that can be achieved in human society does not naturally exist, but we have to create it through discourse and choice. In the third part of his book, Aristotle proceeds to the question, who are the citizens? The decisive remark here is that, contrary to the human body, where the hand never fights the foot, and contrary to the house, where the wood never fights the stone, the city is constituted of elements that fight each other. This puts an end to the more ridiculous comparison between the leader and the shepherd.

The reader will notice that I have been talking about the two possible roads open to political philosophy: the first leaves aside differences and looks for an ideal unity, and the second acknowledges differences and examines the means to realise unity as much as possible. In fact, these two methods represent two options open to human societies themselves. Except for the Greeks in the fifth and fourth centuries BC, and until democracy reappeared first in the United States and then in Europe after the French Revolution, most human societies organised in states seem to have chosen the first method. This method consists in imposing unity by entrusting the sovereignty not to a text, a constitution, but to a person. The images flourish and may be found in all these states: the head, the father and the shepherd – and the subjects are implicitly the feet, the children, the women[6] and the sheep. The names vary: king, emperor, pharaoh, caliph, prince, president, secretary general, and so forth, but the meaning is the same, he is the *dictator* who is in control of everything and whom nothing controls. This kind of government should be described as a theocracy, since the dictator's control is simply left to god . . . or to history! The question now is: what is the function of writing in such regimes? In answering this question, I will be considering Egypt in the first instance.

Writing appeared in Mesopotamia and the Nile valley after the first appearance of administration linked to the first use of numeric signs for censuses, weights, measures, revenues, expenditures, et cetera. This primitive organisation could not develop into a state administration without writing. It is even more difficult to imagine the beginning of colonialism and the establishment of empires without great advances in the techniques of writing. Now it is hard for us to conceive the deep impact the appearance of writing had on people who had never encountered it. A story from mid-nineteenth-century Australia illustrates this impact. It is set in the outback and concerns a coloniser too busy with his herds to visit the city. When he ran out of tobacco, he sent an Australian aboriginal boy to the city with a letter specifying the type of tobacco required and the number of packs. On the way back, the boy could not resist the temptation to steal one or two packs. Of course, the master knew how many packs he had ordered and immediately perceived exactly what had been stolen. The boy was at a loss to understand how a letter sealed in an envelope could have seen his theft. This is the secret of writing: *it sees without an eye and it speaks without a voice*. No wonder that the Egyptians called it 'God's word' ... since it participates in some of His attributes. In a word, *writing is the silent place of Truth*. This applies especially to hieroglyphics since, perhaps more than any other writing, they make you feel the presence of hidden significations behind the visible images, as if they were seeing you without you seeing them. Even today, if you meet a Coptic monk in a desert convent in Egypt, and if he notices that you do not believe completely in the stories of the miracles of his convent's saint, he will tell you: 'This is history, it is *written*.' You get the same assertion from an Egyptian peasant who recounts to you the miracles of the venerated dead *wali* thanks to whom his village became a place of pilgrimage. In brief, when writing appeared, it represented an absolute power as well as an incomparable means of exploitation. Its first use – whether in Egypt, Iraq, India, China or the two Americas – was not limited to such matters as administration, accounting and trade; its main purposes were prestige and the consolidation of power.

The ascendancy of writing was all the more powerful because the people were prevented from penetrating its secrets. The number of the people who could read and write in western Asia and Egypt did not exceed 2.5 per cent to 5 per cent, and sometimes it was even less than 1 per cent. The new technology was the preserve of the ruling class in ancient societies. Its use was supervised by the governing elite whose members were not necessarily able to read and write themselves.

Scribes and priests were charged with writing, but people of higher status dictated the content. Reading was also limited. In the first centuries, hieroglyphic texts were displayed in selected places only: temples, palaces and tombs, where only the elite of the political and religious institutions were allowed to enter. It seems that the display of written texts in public places came later, when the state settled and expanded as empire. Writing was a symbol of political and economic power, writing was a display of prestige, not a means of information. This silent writing widely expanded during the following centuries; laws were engraved on stones in public squares, decrees were written on pillars set in occupied countries, and walls were covered with writing. This 'public' writing had no readers, either because it was in a language other than the one of the occupied country or because it was written in an ancient language that even the people of the occupying country could not understand. It merely displayed the presence of the sovereign everywhere.

The main objective of writing was to maintain the social difference between those who govern and the governed to the point of making it seem blasphemous to think that the first could be in turn governed. That is why the old writings were almost never used for the transcription of spoken languages. Cuneiform writing was first used for the Sumerian language. After the extinction of the latter, it was kept as a writing language during the Akkadian era through which it was considered as a 'grammatical' language, if we mean by that a language that people learn at school and not from their mothers, according to Dante's definition.

Egypt followed the same politics that prevailed in the eastern Mediterranean and which also included the Indo-European peoples in Anatolia and Iran. This politics consisted in having the political power to impose an education in a language other than the spoken one. No one could obtain a position in a political, social, economic or even religious institution without being able to write the 'noble' language. For thousands of years, Egypt preserved hieroglyphic writing with its prestige and divine attribution as a means to express the royal will and public decrees. From the first days of its history until now, Egypt has been known for what an author called its 'linguistic sophistication', that is for its tendency to preserve against change a language considered to be superior to the vernacular and the only one suitable for writing and culture. The literary forms characteristic of the Middle Dynasties era (2000 BC) became a rigid ossified language used for writing literary texts, including maxims, stories or hymns, in addition to religious, magical, medical and astronomical texts – a language thus kept from being contaminated by the people's jargon. Nevertheless, this jargon did seep into the written 'classical' language thanks to the infiltration of love poems and dialogues that had a more subjective character than the other literary genres. The fact that the language of education, administration and culture was not the mother tongue did not prevent some authors from writing in the vernacular and it is no wonder that the mother tongue was particularly popular for love poetry. However, because of the widespread illiteracy, this use of the vernacular did not widen the very limited circle of readers. In other words, things were much the same as they are in contemporary Egypt or were in medieval Europe.

With regard to the demotic writing whose name suggests that it was closer to the people's language, most of the texts we have now are legal documents with formal expressions totally alien to any spoken language. Even personal letters used stereotyped expressions characteristic of public writers' style; indeed, since most people were illiterate they had to address themselves to these professionals, as they still do in some Egyptian villages. By way of contrast, letters written in Greek were filled with chatter and gossip because the sender knew the addressee would read the letter himself and not take it to someone who would read it in public. Most probably, the resemblance found among demotic manuscripts was due to the education system, as we can see from the textbooks used in school. This does not mean that the government in ancient Egypt had the means to control each public writer. The constraint was most probably the effect of an unconscious self-control, in the sense that public writers themselves were under the influence of a fictitious concept of ideal writing.

Of course, the difference between the spoken language and the one used in literature and administration reaches its highest level when a country is submitted to foreign rule. Using writing in literature and on stone monuments was well known in Egypt 3,000 years prior to the invasion of Alexander the Macedonian. Writing was also used for legal purposes such as registering real estate, deciding ownership and contracts, in addition to personal purposes such as marriage, divorce, letters written to the gods, et cetera. It is true that the person who possessed a document to prove his ownership did not necessarily know how to read it, but the important thing was the possession of the written document. Similarly, what was important to the sender of the letter was not the content, but the letter itself, considered as a messenger. To summarise, although most people in Egypt were illiterate and readers and writers constituted a tiny and exclusive elite, writing in Egyptian society was part of all aspects of life; the sense of its importance reached spheres far beyond that of professional writers. Alexander invaded Egypt in 332 BC; of course, demotic writing did not change into Greek overnight – the change took some time, just as Greek continued to be used for some hundred years before Arabic replaced it. What can be drawn from the papyri found up to now is that within 150 years Greek became the main language, at least in the society's highest classes. We are faced with a two-sided phenomenon. Clearly the invaders imposed their language, but we can also say that the fact that the scribes and priests adopted the Greek language was a sign of the elite's flexibility and will to adapt to the new authority in order to preserve their positions and their share of prestige and welfare.

What we have observed so far about Egypt and the eastern Mediterranean is part of a bigger issue to which a good deal of contemporary studies are devoted: that of the relation between writing and power as represented by the state and its apparatus. The state cannot let the texts out of its control because controlling texts means controlling minds. However, controlling texts is also a control via texts. We thus take into account the variety of means to which the state has recourse in order to preserve its hegemony: not only does it have the right to legitimate censorship, requisition, burning and sanction whenever it wishes, but it can also fight any interpretation of the revealed or unrevealed texts different from its own by mobilising the opposition of its *Ulamaa*,[7] corrupting the press and bribing the authors whenever possible. However, if we set aside these procedures, which represent specific contingent operations, and look to the one constant, we can see that it lies in the teaching of writing in a language other than the mother tongue in such a way that the children who learn to write may be said to be nurtured again so as to turn their love to the 'language of the fathers'.[8] The writers are thus brought up as an elite separated from a largely illiterate people. The gap is so large that some of the contemporary 'democratic' states, Egypt in the first place, are so sure of the ineffectualness of writers that, under the pressure of the call to more democracy, they let them freely criticise anything as long as they spare the president who is the totem around which the presumed unity of the people assembles. It should not surprise us to note that the return of democracy to Western Europe after an absence that lasted many centuries was only possible after a long struggle between the common Latin language of Europe and the languages effectively spoken in the various countries.

At this point we are sure to hear some members of the elite say that the vernacular is not suitable for literature because it is a language made for daily dealings and the streets, not for serious thought and deep human feelings. I wish these 'brothers' would think more seriously and understand that writing in the vernacular does not mean using all of the street language, but, rather, extracting a literature from it, a capability which exists in each language thanks to its structure. Do those who claim the contrary know that Galileo, who was the greatest scientific authority of his time, was also the first one to use the vernacular (Italian) in his scientific writings, that he is known for his superb style and that more than one book has been written on Galilean rhetoric? Do they know that his choice of writing in the vernacular and thus defying Latin was the main reason for not revoking his sentence?

Galileo was sentenced in 1633, when the Holy Office, after a six-month trial, declared he was 'vehemently suspected of heresy, namely, of having believed and held the doctrine – which is false and contrary to the sacred and divine scriptures – that the Sun is the centre of the world and does not move from east to west and that the Earth moves and is not the centre of the world; and that an opinion may be held and defended as probable after it has been declared and defined to be contrary to the Holy Scripture'.[9] More than that, investigations proved that the accused not only defended perverse doctrines, but also spread them as widely as he could. In order to achieve this goal, he chose to write in the vernacular, 'Italian, surely not the language best suited for the needs of ultramontane or other scholarship but the one most indicated to bring over to his side the ignorant vulgar among whom errors most easily take hold'.[10]

We previously saw that Dante was the first to instigate the change from Latin as the European unified cultural language to other languages. However, Dante got his inspiration from a previous model, Cicero, who was the first to liberate Latin from its inferiority complex and make it a cultural language at a time when culture was considered as a Greek attribute and could only be expressed in Greek. Prior to Cicero, as he himself said, 'many people who were raised with the Greek culture did not know how to share what they learned with their fellow citizens because they did not think that what they gained from the Greeks could be said in Latin'. Cicero is rightly considered to be the founder of linguistic humanism, calling for the equality of languages as they are all historic phenomena.[11]

The serious awareness of the need to use the vernacular in order to put an end to the esoteric character of culture only begins in the

Renaissance. In large part this was due to the encouragement and support kings gave to nationalisms as a key weapon in their political fight with the Church. A telling example is Charles V asking Erasmus to translate Aristotle. It would take more than a single book to do justice to the full range of this cultural and linguistic struggle. You would need to cover translation from other languages as well as from Latin, the theorising of the importance of the national tongue in Sir Philip Sidney or du Bellay, the writing of grammars such as Alberti's, and the development of dictionaries, this last coming to a certain kind of conclusion with Samuel Johnson. I will just say a word about a translation that may have been the most subversive of all these works; I refer to Martin Luther's translation of the Holy Scripture, which transformed German from a vulgar language into the language of Goethe, Schelling and Hölderlin.

Martin Luther translated the Holy Scripture between 1522 and 1530 because he considered it to be the only text that Christians should read directly, without any screening mediation, be it that of the Church, be it that of such and such an interpreter, or of a language other than the one they speak. Hence the Bible must be translated into a real spoken language. The best dictionaries, according to Luther, are the mothers at home, the children in the street and ordinary men in the markets. The result was a translation full of curses, popular proverbs, phrases impossible to translate literally into another language – the aim throughout being to make men and women feel that God, to whom they ascribed all perfection and majesty, was speaking to them in German. Luther considered himself not as a simple translator, but as the reformer who, thanks to his solidarity with the people's tongue, gave the Germans their language. The translator's competence should be judged on the basis of his knowledge of and affinity with the language he speaks more than on his mastery of the one from which he translates. Now, is it possible to say that Luther succeeded in eliminating all mediation between the believer and the word of God?

One of the highly controversial issues in Luther's translation was a sentence from chapter 3 of Paul's epistle to the Romans, which says that man becomes just thanks to his faith, regardless of his acts. Luther turned this sentence into 'thanks to his faith alone'. The reader will realise the danger of this additional word since it completely eliminates any value attributed to acts, whether good or bad, and this was contrary to the Catholic belief that redemption was possible through acts. What was Luther's answer to his critics? He said they were stupid because, if they knew German, they would understand that when an affirmative sentence is followed by a negative sentence, one should add the word only. A German would say: 'The farmer brought wheat *only*, he did not bring money.' The moral of this story, and the reason I mention it, is that it is possible to eliminate any mediation between man and speech, even God's, except the mediation of the language in which the speech is uttered. As a result, the translation from one language into another, or from the language of writing to the mother tongue, is bound to bring a change in the ways of thought and main concepts, because of the change of the medium itself. That is why a theocratic state will never accept that texts used to assert its legitimacy can be translated into the vernacular.[12]

Of course, democracy did not appear as soon as writing in the vernacular began. This took centuries and the relation between the two is indirect. What is sure is that if writers such as du Bellay and Galileo had not started to write in the vulgar tongue, authors such as John Locke, Montesquieu and Rousseau would not have existed. We live today in a century where science progresses and societies change so quickly that we can no longer wait for decades let alone centuries. This imposes on our writers a double obligation: to write in the language people speak *and* to call for a democracy that truly expresses the people's sentiments and the differences between its classes, not a democracy of 99-per-cent-majority presidents. This double duty is urgent. It is a sad irony that people who get used to tyranny over centuries cannot imagine a regime other than dictatorship. Our compatriots may be heard to say: 'If the government cannot arrest someone, then who could?' Rights are not offered to people as gifts; people earn their rights. They can only do so if writers pave the way for them. Unless Arab writers fulfil their duty today, Arabs will have no existence other than the one the West deems appropriate – if this is not already the case.

This conclusion is based on two observations. The first is that a man who tolerates neither rivalry nor questioning, who rules alone and whose rule is unbridled is generally a man who believes that he is the one who will 'set things right'. This is madness. Any man whose narcissism is inflated to the point where he believes he has 'no equals' has also lost all contact with reality; such blindness can only bring calamity. The proofs of this are innumerable both in the West and in the East, but I will limit myself simply to the history of Palestine. Who can deny the catastrophic failure of all Arab regimes on this question, and their total inability to agree on a common stand towards the Palestinian cause and the Palestinian people? Despite all their claims to unity, despots never agree.

The second observation is that the struggle that started well over 150 years ago between America and Russia ended with an American victory that did not require the use of military force. I say 'over 150 years' because that is how long it is since Alexis de Tocqueville evoked this struggle in his *Democracy in America*. He finished his book by describing the difference of ends and means between the two giants, America and Russia:

> To achieve their aim, the former rely upon self-interest and allow free scope to the unguided strength and common sense of individuals.
> The latter focus the whole power of society upon a single man.[13]
> The former deploy freedom as their main mode of action; the latter, slavish obedience.
> The point of departure is different, their paths are diverse but each of them seems destined by some secret providential design to hold in their hands the fate of half the world at some date in the future.[14]

One should note that if the power is in the hands of an individual or a country, they use it to exploit others. Tocqueville is not defending the *politics of power* but is discussing its *cause*. There is no doubt that exceptional historical circumstances favoured the establishment of political life in America. The Puritans who fled England at the beginning of the seventeenth century established the first political societies in Virginia and New England. Their immigration rate increased year after year because of the struggle for religious freedom and the subsequent civil war in England. Their name reflects their profound and strict attachment to the teachings and rituals of Protestantism. They called themselves 'Pilgrims'. The immigrants belonged to the middle class and enjoyed equality of both cultural and economic resources. It was therefore only natural that they believed in the principle of equality before the law (*isonomia*, as it was called in Athens) and the principles of a republican regime – whereas the political belief prevailing in Europe until the mid-nineteenth century was that republics were only possible in small societies such as cities and the Swiss cantons.

They passed the first criminal law in 1650 in Connecticut. This law was almost a copy of the Law of Moses,[15] which represented God's first word and which was not refuted, according to them, by Jesus's teaching: 'They told you but I tell you ... .' After that, they rebelled against the British Crown and won. Their revolution ended the same year the French Revolution started (1789). There was a real possibility that the thirteen states which had participated in the War of Independence would fight each other once they had beaten the British, but a committee of fifty-five members was formed, headed by

Washington, with Madison, Jefferson and Hamilton among its members. The result was a masterpiece of good sense, intelligence and creativity, whether you consider the application of the principle of separation of powers, which could have taken many other forms, or the cooperation between the state and the federal powers. The legislators' main preoccupation was to apply the principle of the sovereignty of the people, with the most powerful members both of the executive and the legislature subject to election. In addition, the judgement of illegal acts is the business of juries composed of individuals. Citizens are absolutely free to form the unions and associations they desire in order to defend their rights and interests. Such activities can range from a campaign to stop a bus route from passing through a residential street, to mobilising opposition to a particular law, or defending a cause such as abortion, animal rights, and so forth. It is clear that these rights are the best means of preventing conspiracies and armed rebellions. And indeed of opposing terrorism.

To sum up, America's power does not lie in its ships, bombs or even universities. These constitute the power itself, not its cause and source. The source is not its vast lands and the variety of its resources – or Russia would have equalled it – but its constitution and laws. This is the power that enables the United States to buy the economic resources of entire countries and to buy their rulers into the bargain.

Of course, it is too much of a fantasy to imagine our middle-class intellectual elite meeting and writing a constitution with similar objectives that we could use to start our history all over again. Even if they wrote it, it would be meaningless for people who have never had any experience of solidarity in the defence of their common interests and among whom the concept of their own sovereignty without a ruler to govern them only signifies chaos and the end of social life. It is up to our writers to cultivate their fellow citizens on the basis of the principle of linguistic humanism. The duty of writers in our countries is not, in Edward Said's phrase, 'to speak truth to power', for the lust for absolute power entails total deafness to such speech – truth will never be heard while the lust for power prevails – but to enable our peoples to make use of their own speech so that they may free themselves.

Is this another fantasy?

Notes

The first draft of this chapter was delivered to a limited circle of linguists in Cairo. They could not understand that it was not a matter of imposing the vernacular as a written language, but of an archaic state policy which concerns them and which they can change.

1   Claude Lévi-Strauss, *Tristes tropiques*, trans. John and Doreen Weightman (London: Jonathan Cape, 1973).
2   Ibid., 359, 361.
3   Quoted in William V. Harris, *Ancient Literacy* (London: Harvard University Press, 1989), 26; from Diodorus Siculus, xii:13, freely translated.
4   Plato, *Phaedrus*, ll. 275a, b, d, e.
5   For the Greeks, the city was the state and the state was the city. This is a phenomenon that reappeared in Europe during the Renaissance with the establishment of the first city states such as Venice and Genoa. The translation of 'citizen' should be 'member of the city', since this membership entails certain rights and obligations, and constitutes the basis of the political regime. Our current translation, as *mouwatten*, which means literally 'compatriot', is really beside the point.
6   Many jokes and comic stories in Egypt as well as in other Arab countries leave no doubt about the phallic value of the ruler.
7   The religious authorities who decide in cases of conflict of interpretations and who issue the religious decrees. The most prestigious among them is the *mufti*, we may call him the decreeing agent. It should be noted that he is appointed by the head of the state.
8   In so far as they endow the monarch with a fatherly status, theocratic systems may be so durable because they aid defence against the horror of incest.
9   From the judgement handed down at Galileo's trial, quoted in George de Santillana, *The Crime of Galileo* (London: Heineman, 1958), 310.
10 From the Inquisition's report on Galileo's *Dialogue on the Great World Systems*, quoted in Santillana, *The Crime of Galileo*, 246–7.
11 For Lucretius's efforts to articulate Greek philosophy in his *De Rerum Natura*, that is in a language, Latin, that had no words even for such fundamental notions as 'atom' or 'universe', see Patrick Boyde's *Dante Philomythes and Philosopher: Man in the Cosmos* (Cambridge: Cambridge University Press, 1981), 14–15.
12 Most probably the people themselves would disapprove of this idea. I once asked a man who was illiterate if he understood the Koran when he listened to it. He answered: 'Sir, you know, Koran is written in the hearts, you only need to hear it and you are comforted.' It is impossible to exaggerate the importance of Koranic recitations in the Islamic world.
13 In Arabic, there is just one word *quowwa*, which covers the two meanings of power and force – as if political power were a physical phenomenon. There is a word, *sulta*, which means political power specifically, where-from comes the word *Sultan*. But there is no exact equivalent for 'authority'.
14 Alexis de Tocqueville, *Democracy in America*, trans. Gerald Bevan (London: Penguin, 2003), 493.
15 The Pilgrims considered their exodus as a repetition of the exodus of Jews from Egypt and they planned to build a new Israel. No Arab ruler, nor any

member of the elite, would take notice of the deep dogmatic ties between bibliophilic Protestantism and Israel. They prefer to stick to what they know of the strength of the 'Jewish lobby'. More than fifteen years ago, I gave an article to an opposition newspaper about the dogmatic relations between the United States and Israel. It was published – apart from the last sentence stating that nothing will change as long as the Arab regimes are what they are. As the chief editor was a friend, I told him how surprised I was by this omission. He apologised: there just was not enough space for it! It was clear that he had submitted to a tacit and tacitly accepted censorship. Strict limits were assigned that he could not transgress or he would be liable to arrest, or the closure of his newspaper, or both.

7

The Fraud of the Islamic State

The terrorist act of 11 September 2001 provoked two widely different responses. The first, embraced by the masses of both East and West, was the fantasy of the clash of civilisations. The second, embraced by most governments and which could be considered the official view, drew a line between true and false Islam – although no one could tell us the signs by which we might recognise the true Islam. Unfortunately, we are dealing here with a completely different kind of problem from that solved by Archimedes, of distinguishing between a true crown made of pure gold and a false one made of a mixture of gold and silver.

The Koran is God's word. In its written form it is a text. As such, it cannot, as Plato reminds us, answer our questions. It cannot escape the conflict of interpretations. Even if someone, following Ibn Hazm,[1] bans all interpretation and teaches that what is said in the Koran should be taken literally: the 'throne of god' is no metaphor, it means literally the throne of God, words mean no more than what they say – even such a teaching would be an intervention in the conflict of interpretations and, as such, should be considered as being itself a method of interpretation, just as zero is a temperature degree.

As a matter of fact, such a teaching is refuted by the Koran. In surah 3, verse 7, we read:

> It is He who has bestowed upon thee from high this divine writ, containing messages that are clear in and by themselves – and these are the essence of the divine writ – as well as others that are allegorical. Now, those whose hearts are given to swerving [from the truth][2] go after that part of the divine writ which has been expressed in allegory, seeking out [what is bound to create] confusion, and seeking [to arrive at] its final meaning [in an arbitrary manner]; but none save God knows its final meaning.[3]

As noted by the translator, this passage may be regarded as the key to the understanding of the Koran. However, it should be remarked that the Arabic word *muhkamat* that is translated here as 'clear in and by themselves', rather means 'perfectly elaborated', 'impeccable' or 'utterly consistent'. It is not a matter of truth and falsity but of the quality of discourse. Similarly, the word *mutashabihat* which is translated as 'allegorical' derives from a verb which means 'to resemble' and conveys the kind of doubt that a resemblance provokes; it would be better translated as 'vague', 'ambiguous' or 'equivocal', the contrary of 'impeccable'. Once again, it is a matter of the quality of discourse. The question, therefore, arises of how to distinguish between them, between the *muhkamat* and the *mutashabihat*.

No one has examined this question more thoroughly than Fakhr-Eddine Alrazi.[4] He begins by dismissing what he calls the 'verbal proofs or indications'. Because there is no sure sign which tells us whether a word is to be taken in its literal or figurative sense, nor is there a sign to tell us which meaning is intended in cases of ambiguity, equivocation, *double sens*, and so on, it is all a matter of opinion; and opinion, being permeable to falsity as well as to truth, is unworthy of the supreme science, theology. Alrazi therefore appeals to 'intelligible proofs' and 'firm arguments'. But he does not say wherein consist these intelligible proofs and firm arguments. He thus fails to take into account the fact, which he himself had emphasised, that each head of school, refuting the others, claims that *his* theses are based on such proofs and arguments. It is no wonder that Alrazi failed in his attempt to ground faith in a principle intelligible by and in itself. In general, whatever direction they took, Islamic thinkers, and they are not alone in this respect, always came up against this fact which remained unformulated: that there are no starting points for thought outside belief – in science, the starting point is the *choice* of axioms. The conclusion that may be drawn from Alrazi's examination is that *belief, far from being based on comprehension and interpretation, in fact dictates them*. Interpretation may thus be considered as the criterion of faith.

Indeed, except for the Prophet, God did not ascribe the knowledge of the final meaning or of truth to any particular individual, whatever might be his or her status, or to any institution, whatever might be its authority. This is the greatest proof that our relation to God is a relation in which we are answerable to God and to Him alone. Faith is measured by one's discrimination in reading the Koran and one's approximation to the truth. In other words, faith is interpretation and interpretation is the very measure of faith. Herein lies the substance of the notion of *Idjtihad*, which is derived from a root sense of effort, and means 'to try to do the best one can'; an adjective also derived from the same root is mostly applied to students who make a praiseworthy effort in their studies. Just as action is judged according to intention, so faith is judged according to the heart's purity as it manifests itself in 'interpretation' and not in its conformity to a truth that such and such an authority mendaciously claims to share with God. Indeed, to claim to share God's knowledge is as blasphemous as to claim that there are other gods that share God's divinity.

It is precisely on such a blasphemous lie that the Islamic state was built. It was built on the claim that God delegated to it not only His power, but also His knowledge of the 'truth'. Some say that the Prophet had both temporal and spiritual powers. This is false or at best a retroactive illusion. The fact is that the Prophet belonged to a tribal society in which the state had neither existence nor meaning. Far from suggesting durability, the Arabic root *dala*, from which the word used to translate 'state', *dawla*, is derived, has a considerable number of senses which all apply to the ephemeral or what is fleeting. There is no doubt that the Prophet, with his unique relation to God as His messenger, had such authority that people not only appealed to him for advice, but also accepted his decisions without question: his sayings were revelations.[5] These concerned both problems of daily life, such as marriage, inheritance or trade, and properly religious questions such as the rituals of praying and sacrifice. They had *authority* because of the Prophet's unique relation to God. But it would be incorrect to talk of a duality of powers; authority is not power, *sulta*.[6] From beginning to end, the Koran is concerned with what man should be or do according to God's will; it has nothing to do with human politics. We barely find a commandment to obey God, His messengers and 'those among you who are in office', *ouli-l-amri minkum*. And there is no indication of how to put them in office. As a matter of fact, the words for 'office' which are used in this very approximate translation do not mean in any way state office; the phrase may more legitimately be translated as 'your elders'.

Moreover, being the last prophet, Mohammed should properly have no successor, *Khalifa*. However, the first four men who ruled after the Prophet were called the 'shrewd successors', which was admissible because they were among the Prophet's closest companions and had heard the revelation from his own mouth. Indeed, it was one of them, Osman Ibn Affan, who first endeavoured to establish the Koran as a written text. The important point, however, is that it was under their rule that Islam expanded greatly; this expansion made it necessary to create the state. The main founder was undoubtedly Muawiya Ibn Abi Suffian, a rich merchant who belonged to the wealthy part of the Prophet's tribe. His greediness was such that he changed the name of the state treasury from 'the people's money or belongings' (*Malun-Nas*) to 'God's money' (*Malu Allah*).[7] Does not everything belong to Him? What is important is that, as was noted by Ali Abdelrazek and the late Khalil Abdel Karim,[8] there was nothing in the Koran concerning the principles of government. Mohammed's successors were therefore obliged to take the absolute states of Persia and Byzantium as their models. Which meant in fact that under the Islamic state, the relation between the temporal and spiritual power consisted in the subordination of the latter to the former. It was the temporal ruler or head of the state who appointed the judges supposed to apply the Islamic laws, as well as the orators in the great mosques. Men of religion who did not submit to his will were humiliated, tortured or imprisoned.

When Egypt became an Ottoman province in 1517, the Turks accepted the existing social divisions, whether religious, doctrinal, professional or ethical, and they appointed as a head of each division or category a sheikh of their choice. It was in this context that the Ottomans created in 1522 the office of *Sheikh Alazhar*. It was also the Ottomans who created the office named *Dar Al-Ifta' Al-Masriya*; *Ifta'* is the infinitive of a verb that means to decide in cases of disputation regarding opinions or actions. So the name of the office may be translated as 'The House of the Egyptian Lands that says What Is Right in Matters of Belief and Action'. Now, who appointed the *Mufti*, that is the agent of decreeing? It was the Ottoman sultan himself and, at present, it is the president of the republic! What does this mean if not putting religion in the service of the temporal power?

As a matter of fact, rule in the Middle East always drew its legitimacy from some occult superpower with a divine or religious character. This kind of legitimacy results in a system of government based on a total abyss, an unbridgeable difference between the Monarch or the One who governs, to use la Boétie's vocabulary, and his subjects. This difference is not a difference between equal terms like you and me. It has nothing to do with subjectivity and cannot be described in terms of intersubjective relations like the active and the passive, the one who gives and the one who receives, the one who commands and the one who obeys, the master and the slave, and so on. It is not of a dual nature and it transcends reciprocity or exchange, whether of wealth or blows. The place of the monarch is outside the realm of individuals who resemble each other and of the equality of egos. He is a third term to whom we are responsible both as individuals and as egos, while he himself is unquestionable.

You don't need psychoanalysis to see the continuity between this position and that of the father responsible for the family, but from whom no member of the family is entitled to ask for an account of what he does or what he intends to do. To be more accurate about the kind of fatherhood implied here, let us recall that while it cannot be found in reality, absolute or unlimited power can nevertheless be imagined as realised in some figure with which every subject is happy to be identified.

This is the third and final imposture which is our unhappy lot as Arabs. First the people are isolated from the realm of thought by confining writing to a classical language; next they find that state power has usurped God's attribute as the One who 'has the knowledge of the final interpretation'. And finally they are subjected to the imposture of this imaginary father whose truth is pretty well displayed in Garcia Marquez's *The Patriarch*. This means that the idea of the monarch is linked, logically and not merely empirically, to the unity which the community draws from its identification with and submission to the monarch. Anyone so ill advised as to think of expressing a different opinion is considered an outsider; there can be no possible dialogue with them, and the only remedy is death by the sword. That is why the failure of such regimes in fulfilling the main duties of the state, especially political independence and defence of the country's frontiers, results not in revolution but in terrorism.

This structure of power has remained unchanged for centuries. We may find evidence for this assertion in the interview that the president of the Arab republic of Egypt gave to the French newspaper *Le Figaro* in July 2001. Asked about the idea of giving Arafat an honorary office as a president while leaving the real job to a prime minister, he answered that that would be contrary to the 'political culture' of that part of the world. In our countries, he said, a leader is expected to govern. As confirmation, he recalled the example of Nasser. We remember how, after leading the country to its most disastrous defeat in modern history, Nasser announced his resignation on the radio (it is difficult to see to whom he could present it), and how the people poured out into the streets calling for him to come back and not to leave them as 'orphans'. A Middle East leader, concluded Mubarak, either rules or quits. For him, it is a matter of the presence or absence of rule, that is of order or anarchy. It did not cross his mind, nor could it, given the 'political culture' of which he is cynically part and parcel, that it might be a question of the responsibility of government. It is no wonder that, being unable to change him, the people changed his first name – from Hos*n*y, which means 'my beauty', to Hos*t*y, 'my calamity'. To the people themselves, the idea of a ruler whose exercise of power would be submitted to the control of those whom he rules would seem contradictory, if not blasphemous. This brings me to the question put by Etienne de la Boétie in his *Discours de la servitude volontaire*.

We may distinguish two questions in this essay. The first concerns the means which enable a man who is no Hercules, who may even be less of a man than the average, to keep millions of men in a state of servitude. The answer is easy: repression and corruption. The only comment we might make with regard to this is that 'means' does not have here its usual connotation of necessary condition, as in 'physical exercise is a means of maintaining good health' or 'low taxes are a means to an economic boom'. One may be in good health without doing physical exercises and there may be an economical boom although taxes are high. But repression and corruption constitute a sufficient reason for, if not the very essence of, despotism. This allegation enables us to measure the political depth of these notions. 'Repression' does not simply mean the methods of terror which the One uses to suppress opposition. It names a state of things that makes it impossible for the subjects even to think of uniting to defend a common interest. Repression is the foundation of the community and the community excludes civil society. To put it bluntly, I would say that the relation to the One makes of every subject a traitor to his fellows. It is false to assert that the One is put in the place of the third because '*homo homini lupus* [man is a wolf to man]', as Hobbes would say. It is the fact of putting the One in the place of the transcendent lawgiver, or considering him as its representative, that makes a wolf out of a man.

As to corruption, I shall simply recall a television broadcast in which Mubarak addressed a speech to a group of army officers. Among his reflections was the following: 'They talk about corruption, but corruption is everywhere!', the implication being, 'Why should we be an exception?' or 'Why criticise it in our particular case?' He simply forgot, again, that corruption is fought or should be fought everywhere. To him, there 'should' be corruption.

Let us go back to la Boétie, whose second question concerned not servitude as such but its voluntary character. Here lay the mystery for him. It consisted in the scandalous contradiction between the political order and that of nature. Love of liberty is inscribed in the nature of animals, to whom 'liberty or death', that is to say the preference for death over the loss of liberty, is not a mere slogan but a simple expression of their being. La Boétie seems indeed to think that to preserve one's being means to aspire to and defend one's liberty. A creature deprived of all love of liberty would be truly inconceivable. However, men adapt well to servitude; they even seem to call for it. For how could the One, by whatever means, enforce servitude on the millions if they did not somehow call for it, or, to put it in Hegelian terms, if they did not find some satisfaction in it? La Boétie is ready to concede that men still keep a trace of their lost liberty. But the facility with which they put up with this loss and seem resigned to it, even if they mourn it, still remains a mystery to him. Have we an answer to that?

We have already seen how far theocratic regimes depend on perpetuating the infantilisation of peoples through the impudent and fallacious comparison between the One and the father. Such a comparison is open to criticism of a kind that Aristotle put most pertinently. Moreover, the idea of an absolute monarch who draws his legitimacy from religion, which in fact amounts to submitting the spiritual order to the temporal, was submitted to a devastating critique during the Enlightenment. As a matter of fact, inasmuch as it constitutes a virulent attack against absolute government, la Boétie's *Discours* may be considered a precursor to the Enlightenment. It is generally held that it was the philosophical critique of religion which led to the demolition of absolute authority, but we may equally claim that it was the critique of this authority which paved the way to the critique of religion as the alleged foundation of political sovereignty and to the promotion of the idea of the sovereignty of the people. This leads us to the following conclusion: the monarch can only survive as long as he takes every precaution to prevent the transformation of his authority from being an object of faith to being an object of thought. Here the state's policy comes into the picture, with respect to the matter of writing.

The preceding chapters have demonstrated that it was the archaic states' policy of writing that made their authority seem above discussion, not to say natural. The ruse of the state consisted in monopolising the awesome prestige of writing. Substantially, this policy continues to this day. No Middle East ruler will ever accept the teaching of vernacular Arabic in school as a language just as 'grammatical' as classical Arabic. Children with literary talents end up constituting a class whose members are linked together by a linguistic narcissism, as were the scribes. They don't consider the language they write as sacred – but they do think it superior. While there are a few who take a contrary view, to the majority the idea of making a literary language out of the vernacular would seem ludicrous: spoken language is simply not made for culture. One may ask whether such an infatuation is compatible with an authentic education (*Bildung*) of the mind. Indeed, one may consider the main disaster of the Middle

East to be that it never knew the principle of linguistic humanism as reintroduced in Europe by Dante during the Middle Ages and later intensified thanks to the Reformation and to the creation of European nations. The effect was all the more stultifying as the identification of the truth with the written remained unquestioned, contrary to what had happened in ancient Greece thanks to Plato.

These considerations show that the so-called political 'culture' mentioned by the Egyptian president goes further back than Islam and has much deeper roots. Those who want to ground their 'leadership' on Islam merely appeal to a hadith that enjoins us to obey those among us who 'have eminence and authority' (*ouli-l-àmr*). But nowhere is it said that those who have eminence and authority are the politicians or heads of state. They may be teachers or masters in any branch of transmissible knowledge. Maybe more than any other sacred book, the Koran is concerned solely with man's relation to God to the exclusion of any other authority. This relation consists in the faith, of which He is the sole judge, and His judgement, and so, we are explicitly told, is based on the discrimination of the faithful in their reading of the verses. The Koran says nothing about political authority and the ways of government. By an incredible deceit the hadith saying that Islam is both temporal and spiritual (*dunia wa deen*) was exploited in order to submit the Koran to that absolute government. The fact is that when the Arabs built their empire, the models they had to follow, because these were the ones they could see around them, were mainly those of Byzantium and Persia, and therefore they felt they too had to use their own Book as the source of the legitimacy of their authority. But the distinctive mark of Islam is that it is a religion which did not institutionalise itself; unlike Christianity, it did not equip itself with a Church. The Islamic Church is in fact the Islamic State: it is the state which invented the so-called 'highest religious authority' and it is the head of state who appoints the man to occupy that office; it is the state which builds the great mosques, and which supervises religious education; and again it is the state which creates the universities, exercises censorship in all the fields of culture, and considers itself the guardian of morality.

*

I would like to conclude with some words concerning what is to be done.

The contrast described in the preceding chapters between democracy and theocracy does not mean that there is no salvation for us outside democracy. The idea of introducing democracy by the force of arms is ludicrous. You can't make a citizen overnight any more than communism could make the proletariat. Egypt was industralised to a certain degree thanks to some daring entrepreneurs like Tal'at Harb before the Second World War and to Nasser's socialism afterwards. Workers met by the hundreds if not thousands in big factories. But it did not follow that 'class consciousness' percolated down to them from the factory chimneys. The Egyptian worker still goes out to his factory, not to earn his *salary* in the Marxist sense of the word, but in order to get what God may give him – which is the meaning of the untranslatable Arabic word *rizk*. As to our capitalists, given the volume of their wealth, one might compare them very favourably to the rich merchants of the Middle Ages, but they have nothing in common with the bourgeoisie that created industrial civilisation. What is decisive at the present moment is that our despots can no longer exercise their acts of repression safe from view and censure, as was the case only one or two decades ago. For the Soviets to keep the Iron Curtain after the invention of transistors was stupid. Similarly, thanks to the electronic revolution, the world can now witness our citizens beaten in the streets, tortured in the police offices and prisons, arrested by day or by night, blinded by the use of tear gas, and so on. That is what makes it more difficult for Mubarak to suppress the *Kefaya* (enough) movement the way he boasts he suppressed the Islamic terrorists.[9] Such movements of protest are bound to increase, because, whatever may be the illusory satisfaction the regime offers to the people on symbolic and imaginary levels, by dispensing them from *Idjtihad* and imposing its own interpretation through its own religious servants, and by gratifying them with a patriarchal identification, it cannot but engender a real dissatisfaction that grows in proportion to the regime's failure in the economic and political fields. And the protestors will grow more and more daring as they become aware that repression can no longer be hidden from view.

What is happening now in Al-Azhar is a telling example. Al-Azhar is the most eminent university in the Islamic world. The standard of its teaching has sunk lower and lower, as is the case with all the Egyptian universities since Nasser,[10] but its professors are now reclaiming the right to elect the university's rector themselves and they are protesting against the way the *Mufti* (the decreeing agent) is appointed by the president, asking for a new system based on elections. This is an extremely important demand that should be widely publicised and supported by all the world's universities.

Any measure that may strengthen civil society can be considered a welcome step in that direction. Respect for human rights should be observed very closely. Calls for democracy – at least in the sense of a diminished monopoly of power – as well as for the creation of independent universities, the suppression of censorship and the freedom of the press, should be encouraged. Laws that forbid people from defending their common interests by peaceful means – in other words, forbidding the formation of the spirit of citizenship – should be repealed. So should laws that forbid the right to create civil associations, or that restrict them to such an extent as to make them practically impossible. To this we may add a modification of the linguistic policy. Classical Arabic should be taught in schools, of course, but there is no reason to exclude the grammatical study of spoken Arabic as well. Literature in the vernacular should be encouraged in every possible way, and books that attest a remarkable freedom of thought in the Islamic tradition should be published or republished.

This is not a policy inspired by a great ideal; we have seen what happened when a communist utopia was set up to put an end to the exploitation of man by man, and I hope nobody will take seriously the more grandiose ideal of uprooting evil. It is a policy which simply tries to remedy the mischievous effects of a political culture, or rather unculture, based on a paranoid denial of the right and fact of opposition (a denial shared by the 'faithful' rulers as well as the terrorists they breed and who accuse them of being unfaithful). If you wish to be rid of the terrorists then you must get rid of the rulers as well, for the rulers produce the terrorists but are incapable, because of the structures of the state, of getting rid of them.

Such a policy would surely arouse the displeasure of the princes who, among other things, own almost all of the press and publishing houses, and who thus place the great majority of Arabic writers in a state of dependency on their 'gifts'. But a changed policy might also receive a loud echo of support among large sections of the oppressed population, and might bring its salutary results in the long run.

Notes

A first draft of this chapter was written for a seminar on 11 September 2001, held in London on 11 September 2002, under the auspices of the University of Pittsburgh.

1   An Islamic thinker, known as the founder of what may be translated as the 'phenomenal doctrine'. It denies all interiority, whether that of a noumenon or of a hidden meaning.

2 These words are put between parenthesis by me as they don't figure in the original.

3 *The Qur'ān*, translated and explained by Muhammad Asad, Dar Al-Andalus (Gibraltar, 1980), 66–7.

4 One of the greatest scholars of the twelfth century. His exegesis is generally known as *The Great Interpretation, Altafsir Alkabir*. I consulted the edition published in 21 volumes by Al Tawfikia Bookshop, Cairo, vol. 4, p. 160 and following pages.

5 The story goes that the Prophet's smart wife Aïsha said to him: 'O, messenger of God, God sends you the revelations you like to have.' He laughed. The story may be true: women sometimes have flagrant intuitions where men remain blind. But this does not imply that their intuitions are necessarily true; people have to decide for themselves according to their own faith or lack of faith.

6 The notion of authority is extremely problematic in Arabic. As noted before, the word itself has no equivalent. The Arabic word that corresponds to it here, *makana*, refers rather to status. Cf. C. Mansour, *L'Autorité dans la pensée musulmane* (Paris: Librairie Philosophique J. Vrin, 1975). I may simply add that no notion was more dishonestly used in political history than that of *Idjmaa* (consensus), considered as one of the three sources of law, the other two being the Koran and the Prophet's sayings (hadith). Instead of being accepted as a proof of the lack of consensus, every opposition was considered an infringement of consensus, and the opposers were considered as outsiders (*Khawaredj*) who must be physically eliminated.

7 In Arabic, this chapter would be entitled 'Muawiya's fraud'.

8 An Islamist writer who embarked on an 'enlightenment' enterprise, trying to dispel the idealising lies which riddle our political and religious history, and which Islam does not need.

9 In fact, suppressing terrorism in Egypt is not a hard job given that no one can escape the state's eye in the Nile valley; if a terrorist hides in a sugar cane field, the field is burnt; if he hides among his village relatives, the village is destroyed. However, Mubarak's success was relative, since acts of terrorism keep taking place every now and then. It would be more accurate to say that he succeeded in exporting terrorism to the West and other Islamic countries.

10 Nasser started his rule by hanging two workers who participated in a strike in a textile factory, in the name of the revolution's slogan: 'unity, discipline and work'. Afterwards, sixty university professors were dismissed at one stroke and nobody protested: the universities were surrounded by tanks. The students who could remember that the whole of Cairo university went on strike when King Farouk dismissed the great writer Taha Hussein, lost all respect for their professors overnight. Add to this the weakening of both the teaching of foreign languages and the right proclaimed by Nasser of all citizens to have free higher education, and the exponential increase of the population, and you have an idea of the current pitiful state of education in Egypt.

Further Reading

Writing and power

On literacy in the Greco-Roman world, still the most reliable authority:

William V. Harris, *Ancient Literacy* (London: Harvard University Press, 1989).

On Greek law and the history of democracy, the most concise and useful texts:

Claude Mosse, *Les Institutions grecques* (5th edn; Paris: Armand Colin, 1996).

Claude Mosse, *Histoire d'une démocratie: Athènes. Des origines à la conquête macédonienne* (Paris: Editions du Seuil, 1971).

Douglas M. Macdowell, *The Law in Classical Athens* (London: Thames and Hudson, 1978).

On the beginning of political science in Greece (slightly too long-winded, but as compensation contains an analysis both beautiful and profound):

Arlene W. Saxonhouse, *Fear of Diversity: The Birth of Political Science in Ancient Greek Thought* (London: University of Chicago Press, 1992).

On writing and power in general and in the Middle East in particular:

Deborah Keller-Cohen (ed.), *Literacy: Interdisciplinary Conversations* (Cresskill, NJ: Hampton Press, 1994).

Alan K. Bowman and Greg Woolf (eds), *Literacy and Power in the Ancient World* (Cambridge: Cambridge University Press, 1994).

On writing in ancient Egypt, a very general perspective:

J. Baines, 'Literacy and Ancient Egyptian Society', in *Man*, no. 18 (1993), 572–99.

The best edition and translation of Dante's 'Concerning Vernacular Eloquence':

> Dante Alighieri, *De vulgari eloquentia*, ed. and trans. Stephen Botterill (Cambridge: Cambridge University Press, 1996).

On Martin Luther as a translator, and 'linguistic humanism':

> College International de Philosophie, *De l'intraduisible en philosophie, le passage aux vernaculaires*, in *Rue Descartes*, 14 (Paris: Albin Michel, November 1995).

Medieval political philosophy and the first renaissance

The best two books, to date, about medieval political philosophy in Europe and the factors that led to the appearance of new thought:

> Otto Gierke, *Political Theories of the Middle Age*, trans. F. W. Maitland (Boston: Beacon Press, 1958).
> Ernst H. Kantorowicz, *The King's Two Bodies: A Study in Medieval Political Theology* (Princeton: Princeton University Press, 1957).

A book that corrects many preconceived ideas about the Middle Ages:

> Jean Gimpel, *La Révolution industrielle du moyen âge* (Paris: Editions du Seuil, 1975).

A fine book that shows the beginning of the intellectual activity in the Middle Ages and the consequent establishment of universities:

> Jacques Le Goff, *Intellectuals in the Middle Ages*, trans. T. L. Fagan (Oxford: Blackwell, 1993).

On the papacy, the Church and the preservation of Europe's unity after the end of the Roman empire:

> Brian Tierney, *Origins of Papal Infallibility, 1150–1350: A Study on the Concepts of Infallibility, Sovereignty and Tradition in the Middle Ages* (Leiden: Brill, 1972).
> Paolo Prodi, *The Papal Prince, One Body and Two Souls: The Papal Monarchy in Early Modern Europe* (Cambridge: Cambridge University Press, 1987).
> Colin Morris, *The Papal Monarchy: The Western Church from 1050 to 1250* (Oxford: Clarendon Press, 1989).

On the growth of nations and nationalisms in Europe:

Bernard Guenée, *States and Rulers in Later Medieval Europe* (Oxford: Basil Blackwell, 1988).

Etat et église dans la genèse de l'état moderne (Madrid: Ouvrage collectif, Bibliothèque de la Casa de Velazquez, 1986).

Le Sacre de rois (Paris: Ouvrage collectif, Les Belles Lettres, 1985).

A book not to be overlooked, which has been an authority from the day it was published in 1924:

Marc Bloch, *The Royal Touch: Sacred Monarchy and Scrofula in England and France*, trans. J. E. Anderson (London: Routledge and Kegan Paul, 1973).

A crucial book for the understanding of how Europe turned from a 'Christian Republic' or a unified society in which the political and religious powers merged (whether in the form of a political papacy or a royal theocracy), into a political society based on different parties with an attempt to harmonise them:

Max Weber, *Wirtschaft und Gesellschaft, Grundriss der Verstehen Soziologie*, ed. J. Winckelmans, 2 vols (5th edn; Tübingen, 1974); English translation, *Economy and Society: An Outline of Interpretative Sociology*, ed. G. Roth and C. Wittich (Berkeley and London: California University Press, 1979).

Index